Object-Oriented GUI Application Development

Geoff Lee

Autobahn Systems, Inc.
Fremont, California

PTR Prentice Hall
Englewood Cliffs, NJ 07632

Library of Congress Cataloging-in-Publication Data

Lee, Geoff.
   Object-oriented GUI application development / Geoff Lee.
      p.   cm.
   Includes bibliographical references and index.
   ISBN 0-13-363086-2 (pbk.)
   1. Graphical user interfaces (Computer systems) 2. Object-
oriented programming (Computer science) I. Title.
QA76.9.U83L44 1993
005.1'1--dc20

93-4104
CIP

Editorial/production supervision
  and interior design: *BooksCraft, Inc.*
Prepress buyer: *Mary Elizabeth McCartney*
Acquisition editor: *Greg Doench*
Cover design: *Bruce Kenselaar*
Cover art: *M.C. Escher, Print Liberation, 1955*

 © 1993 by PTR Prentice-Hall, Inc.
A Simon & Schuster Company
Englewood Cliffs, New Jersey 07632

The publisher offers discounts on this book when ordered
in bulk quantities. For more information contact:

     Corporate Sales Department
     PTR Prentice Hall
     113 Sylvan Avenue
     Englewood Cliffs, New Jersey 07632

     Phone: 201-592-2863
     Fax: 201-592-2249

Printed in the United States of America
10 9 8 7 6 5 4 3 2 1

ISBN 0-13-363086-2

Prentice-Hall International (UK) Limited, *London*
Prentice-Hall of Australia Pty. Limited, *Sydney*
Prentice-Hall Canada Inc., *Toronto*
Prentice-Hall Hispanoamerica, S.A., *Mexico*
Prentice-Hall of India Private Limited, *New Delhi*
Prentice-Hall of Japan, Inc., *Tokyo*
Simon & Schuster Asia Pte, Ltd., *Singapore*
Editora Prentice-Hall do Brasil, Ltda., *Rio de Janeiro*

Dedicated to my wife, Helen,
and our children, Andrew and Jonathan.

CONTENTS

PREFACE

*R*apid advances of computer hardware and software technology in the past decade have made computers affordable to the masses. Graphical user interface (GUI) is becoming an integral part of application software that runs on various computer platforms. The success of Apple Macintosh computers, the arrival of X Window System in the UNIX workstation arena, and the maturity of Microsoft Windows and OS/2 2.0 running on IBM-compatibles have brought GUI applications to computer users of large installed bases.

Software developers have been moving quickly to take advantage of these de facto standard windowing systems to provide users with graphical user interface applications. For many non-GUI applications, in every imaginable application domain, the popular route to GUI is to retrofit them with graphical user interfaces, which requires much less effort than a complete overhaul does. Existing GUI applications have also can be cross-ported to other graphical environments to serve additional users. When developing GUI applications from scratch, the portability among differing graphical environments is an important consideration.

This book is developed to help GUI application project teams tackle these challenges by offering an approach that integrates the efforts of project managers, system architects, user interface designers, and software engineers. I developed this life-cycle approach over years of teaching graduate-level courses on GUI design and programming at Santa Clara University and heading large software development projects at the leading computer corporations. It addresses GUI application development facing the challenges of multiple-platform support, internationalization, work-group support, and many other real-world requirements.

Central to this approach are high level abstractions of the task model and object model of an application. The task and object models are constructed from users' perspectives to guide the remaining activities of a development project. Using the metaphor of literary or musical composition, the task and object models are like the theme of a GUI application, while the rest of the development effort elaborates on the theme. As the central theme of an application, the task and object models are constructed at the analysis stage. Depending on the requirements of an application and the availability of technology, the design and implementation activities elaborate on the task model and object model to complete the development.

Once you grasp the fundamental concepts of the object model and the task model, this approach can be adapted to the requirements of an application and the specific role of the reader.

ACKNOWLEDGMENTS

I could not have developed this book without the constant support of my wife, Helen, who kept me company on countless late nights. Thanks to my children, Andrew and Jonathan, for their cooperation and understanding during the long period of this project. I owe profound gratitude to God for as apostle Paul wrote, "But by the grace of God I am what I am" (1 Corinthians 15:10 Bibile, New International Version).

I would also like to thank my editor Gregory Doench for his early interest in developing this book and his effort throughout the process, and copyeditor Ruth Frick and Don MacLaren of BooksCraft for their efforts.

Finally, I am grateful to my colleagues at the Department of Computer Engineering for their support in many ways, and to the Santa Clara University for providing a unique teaching environment.

TRADEMARKS

AIX, AIX Interface Composer, Risc System/6000, Common User Access, CUA, OS/2, SAA, and Systems Application Architecture are trademarks of International Business Machines Corporation.

Apple, MacApp, and Macintosh are registered trademarks of Apple Computer, Inc.

Balloon Help, QuickDraw, and ResEdit are trademarks of Apple Computer, Inc.

Borland is a registered trademark of Borland International, Inc.

devGuide, SunSoft, and XView are trademarks of Sun Microsystems, Inc.

Display PostScript is a trademark of Adobe Systems, Inc.

Hewlett-Packard is a registered trademark of Hewlett-Packard Company.

HP-UX and Interface Architect are trademarks of Hewlett-Packard Company.

IBM is a registered trademark of International Business Machines Corporation.

Microsoft is a registered trademark of Microsoft Corporation.

Motif and OSF/Motif are trademarks of The Open Software Foundation, Inc.

MS-DOS and Microsoft are registered trademarks of Microsoft Corporation.

NeXT is a registered trademark of NeXT, Inc.

NextStep, Application Kit, and Interface Builder are trademarks of NeXT, Inc.

ObjectWindows and Resource Workshop are trademarks of Borland International, Inc.

OPEN LOOK and UNIX are registered trademarks of UNIX Systems Laboratories, Inc.

Paintbrush is a trademark of ZSoft Corporation.

Smalltalk-80 is a trademark of ParcPlace Systems, Inc.

Sun Microsystems is a registered trademark of Sun Microsystems, Inc.

Windows is a trademark of Microsoft Corporation.

X Window System is a trademark of the Massachusetts Institute of Technology.

Xerox is a registered trademark of Xerox Corporation.

Autobahn Systems, Inc., has pending patent applications covering the subject matter in this book.

CHAPTER **1**

Introduction

1.1 GRAPHICAL USER INTERFACE APPLICATIONS

Direct-manipulation graphical user interface (GUI) applications allow the user to manipulate graphic objects directly. At the same time, these applications respond interactively to the user's input actions. Two developments have been instrumental in ushering in direct-manipulation GUI (Shneiderman 1992)—the pioneering work done at the Xerox Palo Alto Research Center (PARC) since the early 1970s and the subsequent successful adoption of the technology in mass-marketed Apple Macintosh computers in the mid-1980s.

Desktop publishing applications running under the Macintosh environment have been a major success. Other new applications have also been developed to take advantage of the technology. As graphics display adapters, high-resolution color monitors, and pointing devices have become generally affordable, users of these applications have been able to realize the benefits of intuitive human-computer interaction offered by GUI applications. Pointing devices allow users to interact directly with graphic objects on the display, while high-resolution graphics adapters and monitors allow efficient presentation of graphical information.

Recent development of software-engineering technologies in the areas of object-orientation, rapid-prototyping, and human-computer interaction are making a major impact on the software industry. Although these software technologies are truly revolutionary, they have much potential that is yet undeveloped. The objective of this book is to offer a systematic approach that integrates these technologies for the development of GUI applications.

With de facto GUI standards dominating in their respective market segments, software vendors could capture a larger market share by developing applications that run on multiple platforms. Many software developers have been porting existing GUI or non-GUI applications among different graphical environments. A larger number of non-GUI applications also remain to be reengineered to provide GUIs. We will address these categories of GUI applications development in this book as we present the object model and the task model as the unified high-level abstraction for GUI applications running in multiple graphical environments.

1.2 KEY CONCEPTS OF THIS BOOK

Because the primary objective of this book is to offer an object-oriented life-cycle approach for the development of GUI applications, we have established some simple yet fundamental models as the underpinnings of this approach.

1.2.1 Object-Oriented Task-Analytic Life-Cycle Approach

The life-cycle approach presented in this book treats the GUI application development as an integrated object-oriented software development process. We concentrate on the analysis, design, and implementation activities of a GUI application-development life cycle.

The critical step in an object-oriented software development project is the construction of the object model. In Chapter 5, we introduce a task model based on the GOMS (acronym for Goals, Operators, Methods, and Selection) model, which is well known in the discipline of human-computer interaction (Card, Moran, and Newell 1983). This task model will guide the object-model construction activity presented in Chapter 6 to reveal application objects and the relationships among them (see Figure 1-1).

The object model will guide the life-cycle activities of user-interface (UI) metaphor design presented in Chapter 8, object-oriented GUI design presented in Chapter 9, contextual GUI design presented in Chapter 10, and software architectural design presented in Chapter 11. The task model is also referenced in the life-cycle activities of system-level user interface design presented in Chapter 7 and contextual GUI design presented in Chapter 10.

1.2.2 Unified GUI Application Models

The application object model constructed from the user task model estab-

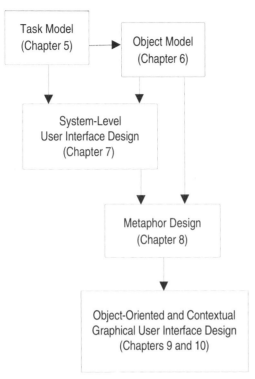

Figure 1–1. The task model and the object model are the underpinnings of an object-oriented life-cycle approach.

lishes a natural and unified representation of a GUI application. We use the same object model in the metaphor design-mapping process, the object-oriented GUI design, and the software architectural design of the GUI application.

When we present the software architectural design in Chapter 11, you will see the application object model is mapped to the software subsystems of the application functional core and the GUI (see Figure 1-2). With the application object model as the pivot, we can control the development process for these separate software subsystems.

The task model, with its roots in the GOMS analysis (very useful in user interface evaluation), embeds the human-computer interaction concerns into our life-cycle approach. Once the implementation activity produces a functional GUI, we can extend our task model into a complete GOMS task-analysis model to evaluate and to improve the GUI design.

1.2.3 Object-Oriented and Contextual GUI Subsystems

As we partition a GUI application into the application functional core and the GUI subsystems, we can further divide the GUI component into subsystems. To present the GUI design as an integral activity of our life-cycle approach, we partition it into the object-oriented and the contextual subsystems.

In Chapter 9, the object-oriented GUI design activity is presented as the mapping of the object model into a vendor-specific GUI style guide. In Chapter 10, we present the contextual GUI design that provides additional dynamic behavior critical to any GUI design.

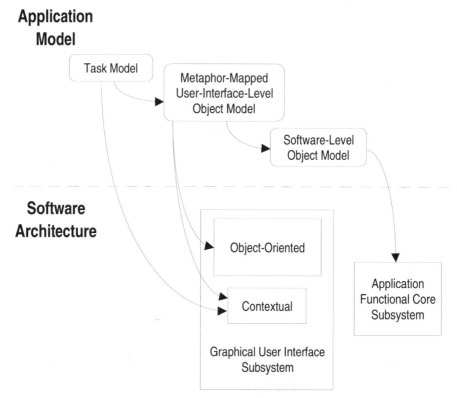

Figure 1–2. The task model and object model are the foundation of our approach.

When compared with the traditional division of presentation and dialog design activities, our approach simplifies the GUI design as a mapping process from the object model and the task model (see Figure 1-3).

1.2.4   High-Level Abstraction Maps to Multiple Graphical Environments

The task model and the object model are the high-level abstraction of a GUI application. With these two models, we can thoroughly specify a GUI application. Developing a GUI for a specific style guide becomes a straightforward mapping process. Regardless of the differences among the multiple graphical environ-

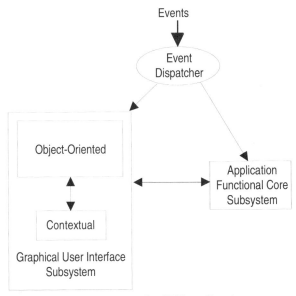

Figure 1–3. Partitioning of a GUI application

ments, the mapping of the object model and the task model into each graphical environment can always be optimized individually (see Figure 1-4).

The traditional approach solves the multiple-platform development problem at the implementation level; this approach frequently falls into the traps of lowest common denominator versus superset argument. The lowest-common-denominator approach supports only functions that can be found on all platforms. The so-called superset solution itself is equally flawed as the lowest common denominator because it introduces unfamiliar elements from other graphical environments into a native environment—a constant source of user confusion (see Figure 1-5).

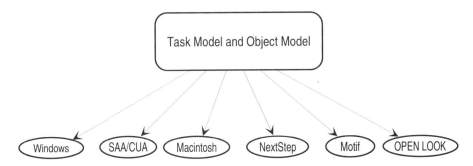

Figure 1–4. The task model and object model are the high-level abstractions equally applicable to multiple graphical environments.

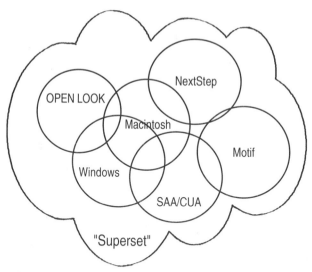

Figure 1–5. Software implementation level approach to cross-platform development.

1.3 WHO SHOULD READ THIS BOOK?

This book is developed largely from my teaching material for a graduate-level course I have taught to hundreds of students over the years. Most of these students are experienced software engineers or managers working in the high-tech industry in the silicon valley. Therefore, if you are a software practitioner or a computer science student, this book should be of interest to you.

Depending on your individual needs and prior knowledge, you can read this book selectively or chapter by chapter. Practitioners can reference the step-by-step presentation of the life-cycle approach selectively. However, the chapters in Part 2 present the fundamental concepts of our approach. Therefore, it will help you to comprehend the material in Parts 3 and 4 if you read Part 2 in sequence.

A standard teaching method in graduate business programs is to study cases. I have adopted this method in teaching my GUI development classes, the cases being the term projects of individual students. Many of these projects are related to the students' work and have extensive scope. The homework assignments are project-milestone reports that match software development life-cycle activities. Individual project-milestone presentation and class discussion reinforce in-depth understanding of key concepts and critical development issues.

1.4 ORGANIZATION OF THIS BOOK

To present a concerted life-cycle approach for GUI application software development, I have organized this book into four parts (see Figure 1-6).

Part 1: Software Development Life Cycle. Part 1 consists of two chapters to introduce readers to the basic software life-cycle approach and an approach for GUI application development.

Chapter 2 describes structured, rapid-prototyping, and object-oriented software development life-cycle activities. In Chapter 3, we present the life-cycle activities for developing GUI applications.

Part 2: Analysis Activities of GUI Application Development. Part 2 focuses on the analysis activities of our life-cycle approach. User analysis, user task modeling, and object modeling activities are presented in Chapters 4, 5, and 6, respectively.

In Chapter 4, we discuss user analysis activity that involves identifying user groups, their computer skill level, and their sociocultural background. In Chapter 5, we present the task-analysis activity that adopts and modifies the GOMS task-analysis model. In Chapter 6, we analyze the task model constructed in task-analysis activity to construct the object model of a GUI application.

Part 3: Graphical User Interface Design Activities. The analysis activities presented in Part 2 are generic to the overall software development of a GUI application. In Part 3, the design activities presented are specific to the GUI subsystem of an application.

In Chapter 7, system-level user interface design activity uses the task model to enumerate task scenarios and to establish the priority of various aspects of the application's object model. In Chapter 8, we present the GUI metaphor design as a mapping process from source metaphors to the target application object model.

We look at object-oriented GUI design in Chapter 9. We discuss the mapping of the object model, with a selected metaphor representation, into a GUI design that complies with a specific style guide.

In Chapter 10, we discuss the contexts, state dependencies, and the modes of a GUI application, as well as a number of essential techniques of contextual GUI design.

Part 4: Graphical User Interface Software Implementation. Part 4 discusses the software implementation issues of GUIs. In Chapter 11, we present the software architectural design for GUI applications, along with a number of software partitioning and layering schemes.

In Chapter 12, we examine several graphical environments and reusable user interface toolkits. We examine the object-oriented GUI toolkits and application frameworks to see thier implication on the software architecture and the implementation of applications.

1.5   A ROAD MAP FOR READING THIS BOOK

If you have prior knowledge in the area of software engineering, object-oriented software development, human-computer interaction, or software architectural design, your knowledge might tempt you to read this book selectively, looking up areas of interest to you. However, we highly recommend that you read it chapter by chapter in the order in which it is presented, especially in Parts 2, 3, and 4. For example, before you read Chapter 9, it is important for you to read Chapters 6, 7, and 8.

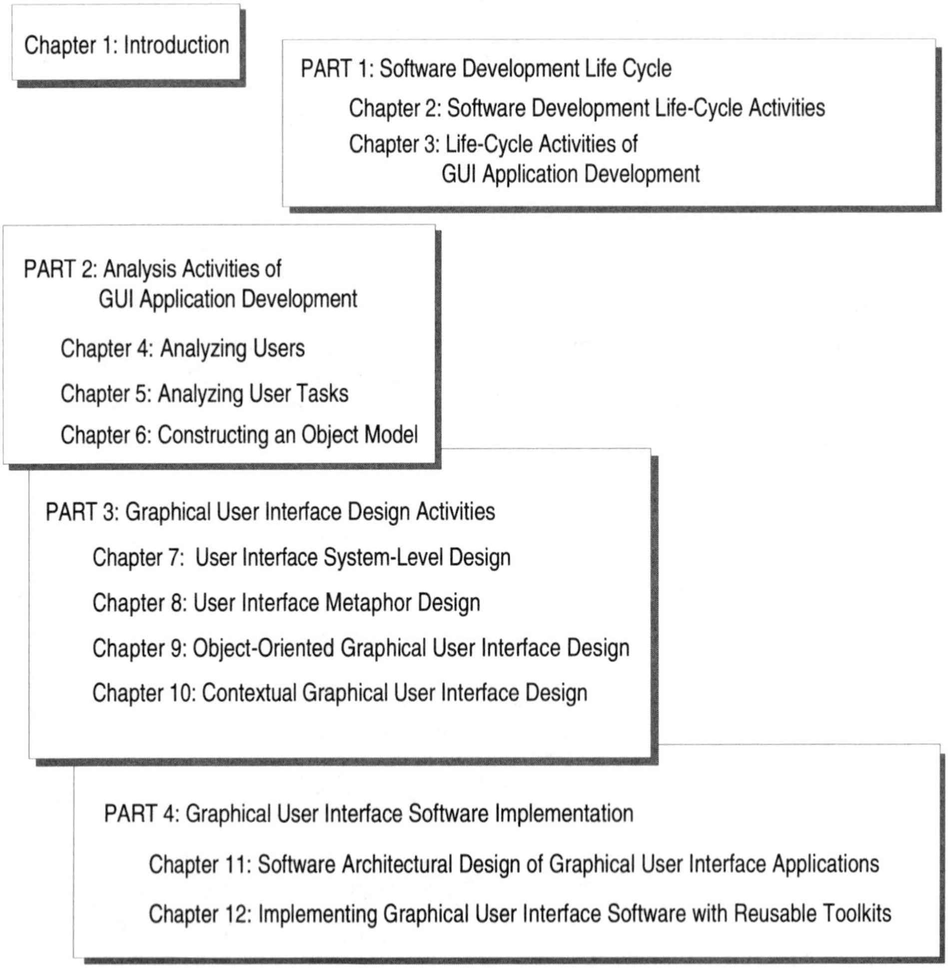

Chapter 1: Introduction

PART 1: Software Development Life Cycle

Chapter 2: Software Development Life-Cycle Activities

Chapter 3: Life-Cycle Activities of
GUI Application Development

PART 2: Analysis Activities of
GUI Application Development

Chapter 4: Analyzing Users

Chapter 5: Analyzing User Tasks

Chapter 6: Constructing an Object Model

PART 3: Graphical User Interface Design Activities

Chapter 7: User Interface System-Level Design

Chapter 8: User Interface Metaphor Design

Chapter 9: Object-Oriented Graphical User Interface Design

Chapter 10: Contextual Graphical User Interface Design

PART 4: Graphical User Interface Software Implementation

Chapter 11: Software Architectural Design of Graphical User Interface Applications

Chapter 12: Implementing Graphical User Interface Software with Reusable Toolkits

Figure 1–6.   Chapters of this book.

SOFTWARE DEVELOPMENT LIFE CYCLE

C H A P T E R **2**

Software Development Life-Cycle Activities

*I*n this chapter, we review the structured approach, the rapid-prototyping approach, and the object-oriented approach for software development. Each of the life-cycle activities of these approaches is first described in terms of generic software development projects. Then we examine it specifically for GUI application development.

2.1 STRUCTURED DEVELOPMENT LIFE CYCLE

The software development life-cycle approach has evolved over the years from the traditional waterfall model to the structured approach (Yourdon 1989). Structured software life-cycle activities may include survey, analysis, design, implementation, acceptance test, quality assurance, user documentation, final installation, and the interactions among these activities. The following subsections describe these individual activities.

2.1.1 Survey

The survey portion of the life cycle involves conducting feasibility studies to identify the users, developing the preliminary scope of the system, and suggesting possible approaches. A project proposal would outline the results of this activity.

Many software development projects originate from customer requests. A customer request may originate from outside in the form of a request for proposal (RFP) document or as user suggestions. Specific requests from various departments within an organization may also result in software development projects.

With the growing popularity of GUI applications, many software projects originate from a need to retrofit existing non-GUI applications with GUIs; to port existing GUI applications to a different graphical environment; or to develop the new GUI applications from scratch.

2.1.2 System Analysis

The primary purpose of structured analysis is to model the application software with standard modeling tools, such as data-flow diagrams, entity-relationship diagrams, and state-transition diagrams (Davis 1990).

When developing a GUI application, the analysis activity focuses on the user and the user's tasks. To develop user profiles, the analysis looks at the user's frequency of use, application domain knowledge, prior experience, and computer skill level. User task analysis uses the task model to describe human-computer interactions of the user performing computer application tasks.

2.1.3 System Design

Software design activity involves partitioning the system specification into logical subsystems (e.g., user interface, networking, and database). For each logical subsystem, the design activity develops appropriate program modules and interfaces among those modules to implement the specification defined during the analysis activity.

For GUI applications, adopting a dialog-independent software architecture would require partitioning the system specification into the GUI subsystem and the application functional core subsystem. We can then develop these two subsystems separately.

In the design activity for the GUI subsystem, we reference the results of analysis activity and adhere to the user interface design principles to produce system-level design, metaphor design, presentation design, and behavior design. The system-level design partitions an application's user interfaces into smaller units. Metaphor design tries to emulate users' familiar concepts in presenting an application. Presentation design is conducted to present sufficient visual information of an application to users. Behavior design is to streamline user-computer interaction and to provide context-sensitive information to users performing their computer application tasks.

There are other possible divisions of GUI design activities. For example, user interface subsystem design activity can be divided into increasingly refined design stages (Foley et al. 1990). Conceptual design deals with the user's mental model of application. Functional design (semantic design) specifies the objects and their information. Sequencing design (syntactic design) defines screen layout and computer-human dialogs. Hardware-binding design (lexical design) defines the details of fonts, colors, and visual cues.

2.1.4 Implementation

The implementation activity involves the actual coding of software subsystems that have been analyzed and designed, and the integration of these subsystems into a complete functional system.

In GUI application development, the implementation activity involves writing programs that implement the designed GUI metaphor, presentation, and behavior; and integrate the GUI subsystem and the application functional core subsystem into a complete functional application. Only at the completion of this activity, the developers and the users will have an opportunity to work with the application and evaluate the effectiveness of user interface design.

2.1.5 Testing

We can start the testing activity when a fully designed and implemented system is functioning. We prepare a test plan to devise a set of exercises for the application software system to perform. These exercises verify that the software functions accurately and consistently conforms to customer-specified requirements. Most of the effort spent in the testing activity involves removing defects that have crept into the system during the analysis, design, or implementation activities.

In addition to exercising the implemented application and fixing any defects we have found, the testing activity also includes conducting an extensive evaluation of user interface effectiveness and consistency. The user interface deficiencies identified during evaluation may result in a redesign effort.

2.1.6 Assessing the Structured Life-Cycle Approach

As we can see from the above description, testing is the only activity in the structured life cycle to allow meaningful user feedback. For GUI applications, finding and correcting user interface deficiencies until testing activity can be costly if extensive design modifications are required.

Since the detailed analysis and design activities in the structured approach may be time-consuming, any user interface deficiencies introduced during the analysis or design activity will have to be corrected later in the development life cycle, which costs substantial resources. This makes the structured approach less appealing for GUI application development, where timely user evaluation and feedback are critical to success.

2.2 STRUCTURED RAPID-PROTOTYPING APPROACH

As opposed to the structured approach reviewed in the previous section, the structured rapid-prototyping approach (Connell and Shafer 1989) does not require exhaustive analysis and design activities before implementation activity takes place. The structured rapid-prototyping approach also differs from traditional throwaway prototyping. An initial prototype evolves into deliverable production-quality software as it undergoes the structured rapid-prototyping life cycle. With its early prototyping activity and iterations of user feedback and developer improvement, the structured rapid-prototyping approach shortens the development life-cycle span, increases user satisfaction, and lowers development and maintenance costs.

The life-cycle activities of the structured rapid-prototyping approach are derived from a structured development life cycle with a number of necessary changes. We can readily apply the fundamental concepts of iteration and evolution to GUI development. Since the objective of a GUI is to allow users to perform their computer tasks efficiently, user feedback throughout the development life cycle tracks user concerns early on. We can improve any deficiency found in a timely fashion without major effort.

The key to a successful structured rapid-prototyping development is access to good software tools that allow rapid construction and iterative evolution of prototypes. Fourth-generation languages (4GL) provide high-level interpretive description of program functionality and are widely adopted for prototyping database applications.

For prototyping GUIs, a number of direct-manipulation user interface design tools are available in various GUI environments. These tools use the source metaphor of graphics drawing applications and are capable of generating software code in 4GL or 3GL programming languages for a GUI design. A production-quality GUI can be iteratively evolved from an initial prototype.

The structured rapid-prototyping approach consists of the activities of rapid analysis, prototyping, design, tuning, and testing. The following sections recount these activities.

2.2.1 Rapid Analysis

In the structured rapid-prototyping approach, the requirements document is produced to specify user profile and the initial user task model to be realized in the initial prototype. The user task model is the essential modeling tool for preliminary user interface requirements analysis; however, the general guideline for rapid analysis activity is not to attempt to specify system requirements in great detail.

We can view the rapid-prototyping process as concentric circles of life-cycle activities conducted with iterations. As the life cycle goes through iterations of user feedback and developer improvement, the initial prototype evolves into a deliverable product.

We use a requirements document to guide the prototyping activity. The goal is to produce something for users to evaluate as soon as possible after the initial interview with users and application-domain experts. Final requirements documentation will be produced as a prototype evolves into a deliverable system. Similarly, we will construct a detailed user task model as the prototype evolves.

2.2.2   Prototyping

In the structured rapid-prototyping approach, the initial prototype is constructed right after rapid analysis activity without going through any formal design activity. The initial prototype is considered a deliverable project milestone. The final delivered software will be functionally identical to the user-approved requirements specification represented by the prototype. Software tools are essential for the rapid construction and subsequent iterative improvement of a prototype.

If we were to apply the structured rapid-prototyping approach to GUI application development, the initial prototype would produce a GUI with presentation and behavior, along with corresponding application functions. The GUI would also reflect an underlying metaphor. However, most of the existing user interface prototyping tools only address the needs of the GUI presentation. The prototyping of the GUI behavior and the application functional core subsystem have not been adequately supported by software tools. The prototyping activity has been limited to the GUI presentation.

2.2.3   Design

In the generic structured rapid-prototyping approach, we derive detailed design from a user-approved prototype. Since a detailed design does not get started until we have finalized detailed functional requirements, we use prototyping as a means of discovering detailed functional requirements. The design activity is mainly a documentation task that provides better structure to an application so that the final product will be easier to maintain.

For GUI applications, a user interface prototype is evolved in the structured rapid-prototyping design activity according to the results of rapid analysis. As users evaluate an evolving prototype, their feedback helps to improve GUIs, and any problem found can be dealt with timely.

Although a GUI prototype allows user feedback during prototyping activities, replacing formal design activity entirely may result in a poorly structured GUI software system even for small scale development, let alone large scale development projects.

2.2.4   Tuning

The performance tuning activity of the structured rapid-prototyping approach involves stress testing a prototype and making changes only when the evolved prototype reveals performance shortfalls in critical functions.

To meet the required performance level, give consideration to the selection of the computing platform, underlying software system, and prototyping tools early in the project life cycle. Some of the user interface prototyping tools can generate highly efficient code; evaluate them judiciously based on your specific needs before making a decision. Since most of the improvements on human-computer interaction issues have been applied as a prototype is evolved, prototype-tuning activity of GUI application development is mainly for correcting any performance problems that result from integrating with the application functional core subsystem.

2.2.5 Testing

As opposed to the structured project life-cycle approach, where the testing activity is the first chance the user has to work with the system, the rapid-prototyping approach uses actual data and user actions to test the prototype as it first becomes available and throughout the life cycle as it iteratively evolves. A prototype has effectively undergone system testing throughout the life cycle as users are continually exposed to the functionality of the system. There is no longer a clearly defined testing activity.

2.2.6 Assessing the Structured Rapid-Prototyping Approach

When a GUI subsystem is the project focus, the structured rapid-prototyping approach can be considered because of adequate support from existing software tools and extensive feedback from users. For large-scale development, it would be inappropriate to replace the design activity entirely with the prototyping activity after rapid analysis; it would also be inappropriate to rely on the prototyping activity to derive designs of user interface metaphor, presentation, and behavior. A more formal design activity is necessary to control those aspects of user interface design activities.

When additional functional subsystems are involved simultaneously in the development, integrating the user interface subsystem with other system functional subsystems constitutes the additional system integration activity in the development life cycle. Without adequate prototyping software tools to coordinate among the functional subsystems of an application, the structured rapid-prototyping approach will be difficult to manage.

To manage complexity and produce highly reusable, testable, maintainable, and extendible software, we can supplement the structured rapid-prototyping approach with the object-oriented approach, which we review in the next section.

2.3 OBJECT-ORIENTED SOFTWARE DEVELOPMENT

The object-oriented approach evolved over the decades from the studies of abstract data types in programming languages (Cardelli and Wegner 1985; Stefik and Bobrow 1986; Danforth and Tomlinson 1988; Stroustrup 1988), semantic data models in database systems (Chen 1976; Smith and Smith 1977; Teorey, Yang, and Fry 1986; Hull and King 1987; Kim 1990), and structured representation of knowledge (e.g., semantic nets, frames) in artificial intelligence

(Minsky 1975).

The object-oriented approach encapsulates data with corresponding operations, and employs polymorphic mechanisms such as class inheritance to allow incremental software development. With data encapsulation, object classes can be conveniently reused, modified, tested, and extended.

As a software development approach, much of the early interest of software professionals has been focused on the implementation aspects of object-oriented software (Goldberg 1984; Cox 1986). More recent developments have focused on object-oriented analysis (Shlaer and Mellor 1988; Coad and Yourdon 1991; Rumbaugh et al. 1991) and object-oriented design (Meyer 1988; Booch 1991; Wirfs-Brock, Wilkerson, and Wiener 1990) activities.

The object-oriented software development life cycle shares some characteristics with the rapid-prototyping approach. Since object classes are abstract data types with encapsulated data and methods, we can regularly refine individual classes while creating new classes through inheritance mechanisms. The object-oriented software life cycle is iterative and evolutionary.

Although GUI applications are the earliest beneficiaries of object-oriented software technology, the development so far has been focused on object-oriented software implementation issues (Barth 1986), which is programmer-centered. On the other hand, the notion of object-orientation in GUI design is user-centered but has been limited to the object-action interaction model—see, for example, the various vendor-specific user interface style guides (Apple Computer 1987; Open Software Foundation 1991a; Sun Microsystems 1990). With an object-action interaction model, a user selects an object (or objects) of interest and then selects an action (or a series of actions) to be applied to the selected object (or objects).

In this book, we present an object-oriented life-cycle approach for GUI application development, using the high-level abstraction of the task model and the object model. Our approach presents a unified notion of object-orientation for both the application functional core subsystem and the GUI subsystem of a GUI application and throughout the entire development life-cycle. The analysis activity involves the construction of task model and object model; the design activity maps the models to a vendor-specific GUI design; and the implementation activity implements the GUI design into software with the help of GUI toolkits or application frameworks and other user interface prototyping tools.

2.4 SUMMARY

In this chapter, we have reviewed the life-cycle activities of various software development approaches. The process of iteration, evolution, and early user feedback in the rapid-prototyping approach, along with an integrated notion of object-orientation for the GUI applications in their analysis, design, and implementation activities, suggest a promising new life-cycle approach, which we will explore further in the next chapter.

CHAPTER 3

Life-Cycle Activities of GUI Application Development

*T*his chapter covers the life-cycle activities of GUI application development in the context of our object-oriented life-cycle approach. Depending on the development approach you are adopting, the individual activities may be scheduled differently, but the overall tasks involved in the entire life cycle will remain the same.

3.1 GUI APPLICATION DEVELOPMENT

By now, you should be able to see some of the unique characteristics of GUI applications. The key to the success of GUIs is user-centered design. With all the software development discipline we can bring with the structured approach, its late user feedback is inappropriate for developing GUI applications.

The structured rapid-prototyping approach allows ample opportunities for user feedback throughout the development life cycle, which is a major advantage for developing GUIs. There are also a number of software tools for rapidly building user interfaces in various GUI environments. However, without support for object-orientation, their contribution to the overall development effort is not far-reaching enough, especially in cases where they need to be extended beyond a limited set of supported GUI interaction components, or where they need to systematically manage hierarchies of user interface templates for large applications. The lack of disciplined design activity in the structured rapid prototyping approach is also inappropriate for the extensive design activities required in GUI applications.

The notion of object-orientation in GUI application development has been limited to object-oriented programming, which is programmer-centered instead of user-centered. It focuses on the systematic composition of GUIs from an existing class library, which is much more efficient than developing them from scratch.

Not to be hindered by the limitation of these existing approaches in GUI application development, we have devised an integrated object-oriented life-cycle approach to satisfy the unique requirements of user-centered design in GUI applications. The life-cycle activities of our approach include user analysis, user task analysis, and object-oriented analysis; system-level design, metaphor design (mental model to help users comprehend the application), object-oriented GUI design (spatial layout of user interface interaction components and temporal sequences of computer-human interaction), and contextual GUI design (visual cues, and context-sensitive information); software prototyping with object-oriented toolkits or application frameworks and other prototyping tools; and evaluation of the effectiveness of GUI designs.

3.2 PRELIMINARY REQUIREMENTS SPECIFICATION

A software project initiated by organizations comes in the form of request for proposals, a brief problem statement, or a detailed requirements specification. Regardless of its format, the purpose of the requirements specification is to communicate to all parties involved in the development project a set of agreed-upon objectives, features, and constraints. Explicit statements and clear specification convey to the customers what they can expect; and, to the developers, what they need to accomplish.

A project life cycle begins with the activity of analyzing the requirements specification; and, in the final customer acceptance testing, the deliverable system is verified against the requirements specification. Although we can measure project performance by several criteria, customer satisfaction is always the key indicator when project deliverables meet requirements specification, on schedule, and within budget.

Differing life-cycle approaches would allow a varying degree of freedom in iterating or subtasking life-cycle activities. A requirements specification itself may also undergo several revisions throughout a project life cycle and remains the primary project documentation. As we will see later in this chapter and in the next chapters, the statements in the requirements specification provide critical input to the analysis activities. Regardless of the life-cycle approach used in a project, a preliminary requirements specification should contain the following sections:

1 **Objectives:** Objective of a project should be clearly stated in this section. The purpose of an application software development project is to help users perform certain tasks. Requirements documentation specifies "what" needs to be accomplished in a project.

2 **Features:** To perform their tasks, users invoke various features that are supported by the application software. For example, word-processing application features include backing up files automatically, spell checking, indexing, preparing tables of contents, page numbering, and so on. Required features are intended to improve user's task performance. They also affect overall software design and implementation effort. Furthermore, salient features are often the major factors differentiating your application software from that of a competitor.

3 **Constraints:** The constraints section specifies the hardware and software environment, standards compliance, and other performance-related issues. These constraints can be based on the customer's organizational considerations. An organization moving to standardize its computing environment would require that the software developed run under the same environment. If a more powerful hardware or software environment is necessary to achieve a performance objective, the customer would require transparent implementation of some form of gateways to accommodate the existing computing environment. Standards compliance often prevents the customers from getting locked into proprietary solutions. A standard can originate from a consortium effort such as X Window System, which has been widely adopted by computer workstation vendors, or from an industry de facto standard such as Microsoft Windows on personal computers. With a standard hardware and software environment, large number of off-the-shelf software tools and utilities are also readily available, and this helps lower development effort and cost.

3.3 GUI APPLICATION ANALYSIS

Four types of analysis are necessary for GUI application development—user requirement analysis, user analysis, user task analysis, and object-oriented analysis. User requirement analysis specifies general criteria of the computing hardware/software environment, functional requirements, and acceptable performance level. User analysis segments user groups with the criteria of use frequency, application-domain knowledge level, computer skill level, and so on.

Task analysis decomposes user tasks into goals and associated methods, operators, and selection rules. Object-oriented analysis constructs the object model for
the application.

3.4 GUI DESIGN

Task analysis revealed extensive in-depth information (priorities of object
model elements) for designing and evaluating user interfaces. Prioritizing and
grouping of objects, attributes, and operations are done in the system-level user
interface design activity. User analysis provided clues to the user's previous
experiences which help us devising user interface metaphors. Presentation
design and behavior design are the spatial and temporal aspects of object-oriented GUI design. The optimal design requires minimum screen real estate and
user input actions. In the stage of contextual GUI design, visual cues and contextual messages are added to further refine the GUI.

3.5 GUI PROTOTYPING

Although it would be more flexible to defer user interface style-specific
activities as late as possible in the development life cycle of portable GUI applications, most commercial GUI prototyping tools are specific to certain GUI environments. In order to take advantage of these existing tools, prototyping activity
will have to be done in a specific GUI environment.

GUI prototyping tools themselves are direct-manipulation GUI applications. They support the composition of GUI presentation from a set of GUI interaction components selectable from a palette. Other aspects of the GUI will have
to be manually coded. Results of design activity guide the creation of a prototype
that contains user interface presentation, behavior, visual cues, and contextual
messages. Subsequent evaluation activity provides user feedback to direct necessary modifications in user interface priorities, metaphors, presentation, behavior, visual cues, and contextual information.

GUI prototyping tools alone are usually insufficient for large complex GUI
applications. With object-oriented toolkits or application frameworks, we can
extend class libraries through inheritance mechanisms. Systematic GUI composition with extendible object-oriented toolkits or application frameworks allows
more comprehensive prototyping of designed GUIs.

3.6 GUI EVALUATION

As the prototype becomes available, users can start working with the prototype and evaluate the effectiveness of its GUI. User feedback leads to improvement of GUIs. From actual user-computer interaction, a user task analysis
model can be refined and completely documented. As user interface metaphor is

reflected in the GUI prototype, user evaluation can also reveal potential meta-phor mismatches that deviate from users' mental model of the application. We can correct these with better metaphor design or by designing preventive user interface behavior to minimize possible user errors (e.g., provide undo/redo, context-sensitive help, and error recovery mechanisms).

3.7 GUI APPLICATION INTEGRATION

After being developed separately from the application functional core sub-system, the life-cycle activities concentrate on going through iterations of design-ing, prototyping, and evaluating GUIs. At some point, we would need to continue to the next stage and integrate the GUI subsystem with the application func-tional core subsystem. Only after integration will we have a fully functional GUI application. Applications with extensive output graphics generated from applica-tion functional core subsystem will have to make sure the two way communica-tion works correctly. Additional life-cycle iterations can be repeated if any deficiency is found.

3.8 SUMMARY

In this chapter, we have examined an object-oriented life-cycle approach for developing GUI applications. In the remaining parts of this book, we will present the individual life-cycle activities of analysis for the application, design for GUI, and implementation for GUI prototying and software integration. Although we don't cover the evaluation activity in this book, the findings from this activity can be easily incorporated into the next iteration of other life-cycle activities.

ANALYSIS ACTIVITIES OF GUI APPLICATION DEVELOPMENT

C H A P T E R   **4**

Analyzing Users

*T*he user should be the primary concern throughout the development of a GUI application. We unfold our object-oriented life-cycle approach with the activity of user analysis. The purpose of this activity is to find out who the target users are, what roles they have, what skill levels they possess, and how they will use the application. First we present some common analysis factors: user's organizational role, computer skill level, application-domain skill level, usage pattern, and social/cultural background. Then we present a procedure to identify analysis factors specific to individual applications and distinct user groups. We will use a personnel recruiting application to demonstrate the analysis process.

4.1 OVERVIEW

The pioneers of computer-human interfaces have emphasized over the years the importance of user-centered design (Norman 1988). You will see as we proceed in this book that a clear understanding of users' needs early in the development life-cycle will help you deliver a highly usable product.

User analysis identifies factors critical to an application and then segments users into distinct user groups. Each distinct group of users shares a set of similar characteristics. The challenge of a development project is to accommodate the needs of various target user groups while minimizing development effort and future maintenance cost.

4.2   USER ANALYSIS FACTORS

In the following sections, we examine the common analysis factors of user roles, organizational differences, social/cultural background, computer skill level, application-domain skill level, and usage pattern. The implication of these factors on an application development, along with relevant examples, are examined.

4.2.1   Roles

A job position and its accompanying responsibility characterize a user's role in an organization. The specific roles of users are defined by the tasks they perform. Customization of user interface design based on a user's role improves usability while guiding design decisions in our object-oriented life-cycle approach.

If you look around in any organization, you'll find that it consists of people working together in a structured manner. The structure of an organization defines the relationships among people. People assume a specific position in an organization to maintain such structured relationships.

As software development moves toward integrated and collaborative computing, a team of users with different roles may be working together to accomplish organizational goals. For example, in an integrated software-engineering application, a project manager performs various project scheduling and resource allocation functions, while the project team members perform their individual assignments, individual task scheduling, and status reporting functions.

In user interface application development, the immediate implication of different user roles is the different tasks they will perform. Some of these tasks may overlap among different user roles, and some of them may be exclusively for specific user roles. Since we are taking an object-oriented approach in this book, we look beyond the user tasks to identify application objects that may be shared among user roles, or that are exclusively for a certain user role, as depicted in Figure 4-1.

4.2.2   Organizational Differences

Different organizations may have very different structures and relationships among their people in order to accomplish their goals. Depending on the application domain, there can be many notable differences in job functions as

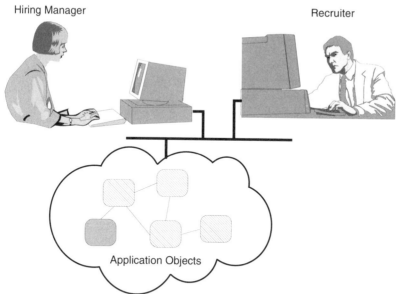

Hiring Manager   Recruiter

Application Objects

Figure 4–1. Multiple user interfaces for different user roles to access the application objects.

well as differences in the scope of function for the same position.

E X A M P L E   4 – 1

A software project manager of a small project team has the responsibility of project scheduling, schedule tracking, system architectural design, and software coding functions. Another software project manager of a large development project may be responsible for only the project scheduling and project tracking functions. However, while the functions of project scheduling or project tracking might be the same, in the larger project they will have larger scope than they do in the smaller project. Project-management software for the smaller project has to be versatile, but can be a single-user version, with smaller computing resource requirements. On the other hand, the larger project requires project-management software with multiuser support and larger computing resource requirements.

An organization may also reorganize periodically to remain competitive and productive. Reorganization may involve changing goals, structure, or people. As a result of a reorganization, the functions of a position and the scope of each function may change accordingly.

E X A M P L E   4 – 2

An accountant in a small accounting department has the responsibility of handling payroll, accounts receivable, and accounts payable. As the organization grows, the accountant's workload gets heavier. The accounting department undergoes reorganization to eliminate the payroll function by hiring an outside payroll service. It divides the accounts receivable and accounts payable functions into two positions. A new accountant is hired to handle accounts receivable, while the original accountant continues to handle accounts payable.

The immediate implication of this reorganization in terms of departmental computing needs is the necessary upgrade of single-user accounting application software to allow multiple user access.

4.2.3   Computer Skill Level

A user must possess several general computer skills to use a GUI application. We measure users' computer skills by their proficiency in using input devices (e.g., mouse, keyboard) and their familiarity with the interaction model of a GUI environment. A user can acquire computer skills from previous experience with other GUI applications or from using an application frequently.

We can segment the user's computer skill level into the levels of beginner, novice, experienced, and expert:

1 **Beginner:** Beginners have little knowledge of a GUI environment or of how to use input devices to interact with a computer. They need extensive learning aids (e.g., on-line help and tutorial) and slower-paced visual information updates for applications performing such functions. The learning aids instruct users on how to interact with a GUI application and the overall GUI environment.

2 **Novice:** Novice users have some experience using computer applications, although they may not be familiar with a specific GUI environment. With limited computer skill, they may make many mistakes interacting with GUIs. They also need to use the same learning tools as beginning users do.

3 **Experienced:** Experienced users have considerable experience with GUI applications. Novice users become experienced if they use an application frequently to get more practice. Experienced users don't require extensive support as novice users do and would prefer faster interaction with an application.

4 **Expert:** Expert users have extensive experience with a number of GUI applications. They need a sophisticated user interface that provides shortcuts. Expert users achieve high performance by navigating with shortcuts and by having faster interaction with an application.

4.2.4   Application-Domain Skill

Another important users' skill is the level of their application-domain knowledge. As an application is developed to help users perform their tasks, the users themselves must have sufficient knowledge of the tasks they perform and how to perform them. For many professional applications, such as an electronic design-automation tool or a computer software-engineering tool, a user's application-domain skill can be acquired only through years of formal training. It is important for a professional application to present a mental model based on application-domain knowledge.

We can divide a user's application-domain skill into the following four levels:

1 **Beginner:** Beginners have no previously knowledge of an application domain. They need extensive learning aids that provide instructions on how to perform application-specific tasks, which are very different from the common computer interaction skills for graphical environments. An application should also provide generous status information to guide beginners throughout their application sessions. Clearly stated error-recovery hints should also be provided to help beginners recover from mistakes which will most likely be numerous.

2 **Novice:** Novice users have some application-domain knowledge. However, they may still make many mistakes performing application tasks. They may need to use the same learning tools as beginners do.

3 **Experienced:** Experienced users have considerable application-domain knowledge. They have good understanding of how to perform application tasks with an application.

4 **Expert:** Expert users have extensive application-domain knowledge. They devise new ways of performing application tasks. They also need sophisticated facilities that allow them to modify and extend the capabilities of a domain application.

4.2.5 Application Usage Pattern

Depending on an individual's pattern of using a GUI application, that individual's computer skill level changes over time. The more frequently he or she uses an application, the better the user gets with computer skill level. We can divide users' usage patterns into the following two categories:

1 **Occasional user:** Occasional users don't advance their computer skills over time. They maintain the same skill level or may even lose skills over time because of their lack of practice.

2 **Frequent user:** Frequent users get a lot of practice over time. Their computer skill levels also advance over time, while their reliance on learning aids and contextual help decreases and their use of sophisticated interaction skills increases.

4.2.6 Sociocultural Differences

Every culture has its unique mix of language, religion, arts, beliefs, and other behavioral patterns that have evolved over the years. As business, arts, and other human activities transcend the boundary of nations' borders, many software applications have also been marketed worldwide. With textual and graphical information access and presentation capability in the GUI applications, localizing software for different countries involves supporting native languages and localizing user interface designs when necessary. Even countries speaking the same language can use different expression and terminology in various circumstances.

The GUI design may have to be extensively modified in order to accommodate users from different cultures. For example, in Western-language-speaking countries, visual scanning is done horizontally from left to right; in some Asian countries (e.g., China, Japan, Korea), visual scanning can be done either vertically from right to left or horizontally from left to right; in Arabic and Hebrew languages, visual scanning is done horizontally from right to left. We may also have to use different user interface metaphors for an application supporting multiple cultures.

4.3   PROCEDURE FOR CONDUCTING USER ANALYSIS

A brief description of intended users in a preliminary requirements specification will get us started on the task of user analysis. Through interviewing users, we can gather important information for further analysis. Once we have sufficient information about target users, we take the following steps to conduct the activity of user analysis:

4.3.1   Identify Analysis Factors Critical to Application

Examine the user information to identify the factors critical to the application.

EXAMPLE   4 – 3

Preliminary requirements: *A single-user accounting application is developed to target small accounting firms in the U.S. market.*
There are a number of key statements in this preliminary requirements specification that imply the relative importance of some of the analysis factors.

•*"A single user"* implies only one user role, which can then be excluded in the analysis.
•*"small accounting firm"* further implies the organizational characteristics to be smaller-sized.
•*"in the U.S. market"* indicates a homogeneous cultural background of users.

This leaves only the factors of user computer skill level, application-domain skill level, and usage pattern as the critical factors to be analyzed.

4.3.2 Discover Other Factors Critical to Application

There are many other possible factors that may turn out to be critical to an application. Try to discover additional factors to improve the results of user analysis.

E X A M P L E   4 – 4

In the above example, the preliminary requirements did not mention the target computing platform. In reality, users may have their preferred GUI environment. Considering this factor is critical to the application.

4.3.3 Estimate Distribution of Users of Each Application-Critical Factor

Find the distribution of users for each possible user group under the application-critical factors. A careful user survey should provide us with such information.

E X A M P L E   4 – 5

Continuing with the same example, the estimation of user distribution follows.
Computer skill level:

Beginner	15%
Novice	30%
Experienced	45%
Expert	10%

Application-domain skill level:

Beginner	5%
Novice	15%
Experienced	50%
Expert	30%

Usage pattern:

Occasional user	20%
Frequent user	80%

Preferred graphical environment:

Windows 3.x	50%
Macintosh	35%
Other	10%
Don't know	5%

4.3.4 Rank Distribution to Identify Major User Groups

If the previous step reveals fairly concentrated distribution of user groups, we can skip to the next step. However, if the target user groups are loosely spread and fragmented, we need to analyze the distribution further. The distribution ranking is significant for individual analysis factors, as well as for the combination of analysis factors. The probability of a user having a combination of characteristics is the product of individual distributions. The higher values of probability indicate the characteristics of major user groups.

E X A M P L E   4 – 6

Continue examining the accounting application example; to find the possible number of combinations of a set of characteristics, multiply the number of subgroups in each critical analysis factor:

$$4 \times 4 \times 2 \times 4 = 128 \qquad\qquad (1)$$

The overall ranking of combined characteristics is listed in Table 4-1.

Table 4–1 Distribution Ranking of User Groups

Computer Skill	Application-domain Skill	Usage Pattern	Preferred Platform	Probability(%)
experienced	experienced	frequent	Windows 3.x	9.00
experienced	experienced	frequent	Macintosh	6.30
novice	experienced	frequent	Windows 3.x	6.00
experienced	expert	frequent	Windows 3.x	5.40
.				
.				
.				
expert	beginner	occasional	don't know	0.05

As we can see in the table, a user is most likely to be experienced in computer and application-domain skills, frequently using the application on a Windows 3.x or Macintosh platform. Along with other top-ranked combinations, they reveal the dominating characteristics of users.

4.3.5   Analyze the Collective Implication of User Distribution

The previous steps have identified user groups and their characteristics. With limited project resources, it is impossible to address the specific needs of every conceivable individual user; but satisfying the needs of major user groups is crucial to the success of an application. With a specific user distribution, there are many implications in the subsequent life-cycle activities.

E X A M P L E   4 - 7

In the example of an accounting application, the distribution of users under various analysis factors has the following implications:

1 Looking at the usage pattern, 80% are frequent users, 10% are beginners, and 35% are novice computer skill level users. With frequent usage, the users with lower computer skill levels will become experienced users. When the beginners and novices begin learning to use an application, they will need extensive support. As they become experienced or even expert users, extendibility and alternative task scenarios become important.

2 Under the factor of application-domain skill level, 50% are experienced and 30% are expert users. With a high percentage of users very knowledgeable of the application domain, the metaphor mental model to be constructed during metaphor design (covered in Chapter 8) should allow users to apply their application-domain knowledge.

3 The user distribution for the analysis factor of preferred graphical environment showed 50% Windows 3.x preference and 35% Macintosh preference. The distribution is related to the analysis factor of computer skill level, such that the users' computer skills are specific to certain GUI environments. To allow the majority of users to take advantage of their existing computer skill on a GUI environment, we need to develop two GUIs for the application, with one adhering to the Windows interface application design guide (Microsoft 1992) and another conforming to the Apple Macintosh human interface guidelines (Apple Computer 1987, 1991).

4.4 CASE STUDY: A PERSONNEL RECRUITING APPLICATION

In this section, we apply the user analysis procedure to a personnel recruiting application to find out the critical analysis factors and the implications of these factors.

The preliminary requirements are:

An application software needs to be developed to integrate the corporatewide recruiting process as much as possible. The personnel recruiters, hiring managers, and any other staff involved in the recruiting process will be able to communicate with each other through the application using a number of desktop computing environments.

We follow the procedure presented in the last section to analyze the target users.

1 **Identify analysis factors critical to the application.**

Quick analysis of the commonly used analysis factors finds that the user roles, computer skill level, application-domain skill level, and usage pattern are the critical analysis factors. The factors of organizational and cultural differences are beyond the scope of this custom application.

User roles are particularly important for this application. Within the target organization, there are three different user roles collaborating in the recruiting process.

•**Personnel recruiters** handle several job-opening requests simultaneously, respond to the requests from hiring managers, manage recruiting channels, interact with job applicants, and schedule job interviews.

•**Hiring managers** specify the requirements of an open position and work with personnel recruiters to fill an open position in their departments.

•**Other hiring committee members** may be involved in the interview process to evaluate the qualification of candidates.

2 **Discover other factors critical to the application**.

We have found no other significant analysis factors for this application.

3 **Estimate the distribution of users of each application-critical factor.**

Each personnel recruiter works with three hiring managers on average. The hiring managers also let two of their staff get involved in the hiring process.

User roles:

Personnel recruiter	10%
Hiring manager	30%
Other hiring committee member	60%

This company has several departments that are computerized, but there are still departments with limited computing resources.

Computer skill level:

Beginner	10%
Novice	30%
Experienced	50%
Expert	10%

From the distribution of user roles, we can tell that personnel recruiters are very familiar with the recruiting process; some hiring managers are more experienced in the recruiting process; while other hiring committee members are usually unfamiliar with the entire hiring process.

Application-domain skill level:

Beginner	50%
Novice	30%
Experienced	20%
Expert	10%

The personnel recruiters constantly respond to hiring managers' requests to fill open positions, so they will use the application frequently. For individual hiring managers, filling an open position is only an occasional task.

Similarly, other hiring committee members rarely get involved in the recruiting process.

Usage pattern:

Occasional	90%
Frequent	10%

4 Rank the distribution to identify major user groups.

Analyzing the user distribution of individual factors, we found that the key factor is user roles, and other distributions have a high correlation with this factor. The three major groups of users are based on the three different user roles.

•Other hiring committee members are more likely to have novice- or experienced-level computer skills, beginner-level application-domain knowledge, and occasional usage.

•The users in the hiring-manager group are more likely to be at the experienced computer skill level, novice or experienced application-domain skill level, and the occasional use category.

•The personnel recruiters are more likely to be experienced computer users, having expert-level application-domain skill, and being frequent users of a recruiting application.

5 Analyze the collective implication of user distribution.

Examining the three major user groups, we see that the personnel recruiters are frequent users even if they are not the majority users. The main purpose of this application is to help personnel recruiters in doing their job, which includes their professional tasks of managing recruiting channels, responding to job applications, and scheduling interviews. With this in mind, we should develop a modular application that allows recruiter-specific tasks to be performed by expert users. The metaphor mental model should follow closely with the application-domain knowledge.

The majority of users will be hiring managers and other hiring committee members. Although they use the application only occasionally and are not knowledgeable of the application domain, they only have to perform a limited number of tasks throughout the recruiting process. We should develop specific modules of this application to handle the fewer tasks they perform. These modules should provide extensive support for beginner and novice users, as well as a metaphor mental model that accommodates users with different application-domain skills.

4.5 SUMMARY

There are many factors that can be used to characterize users. We have described only some of the commonly used factors in this chapter. Depending on the requirements of individual applications, we can discover other critical factors to segment user groups. It is important to recognize the characteristics of differing user groups and to try to tailor the application to the needs of each group.

In presenting the procedure to analyze users, we have tried to keep it simple and practical. But a developer must work closely with application-domain experts and target users to interpret correctly user characteristics and to identify user groups.

As we proceed with the subsequent life-cycle activities, the information provided by user analysis will help us to make critical modeling and design decisions. For example, in Chapter 5, we emphasize the significance of user roles in task modeling, which will lead us to identifying application objects specific to each user role in Chapter 6.

4.6   BIBLIOGRAPHIC NOTES

Several research papers have offered techniques to accommodate user differences in user interface applications. The individual differences of users are discussed, and the implication of individual differences and ways to accommodate them are also presented (Egan 1988; Mayer 1988). In these references, you can find discussion of various research results on a number of analysis factors, such as users' age, technical aptitudes, and personality. There are also in-depth discussion and an extensive list of references if you are interested in further study of the psychological aspects of user differences, which we have kept to the minimum in our presentation.

CHAPTER **5**

Analyzing User Tasks

Task analysis helps the user interface software developers to envision an application from a user's perspective. It is important to uncover user task-performing information early in the development life cycle.

First, to introduce our task-analysis approach to you, we review the GOMS task model. The GOMS task analysis is highly structured and comprehensive in examining user task performance. However, a lot of the detailed information required by the GOMS task analysis can only be collected after we have designed and prototyped a user interface.

In the second section, we simplify the GOMS model. This changes it from a design-improvement tool (its original intended purpose) to a tool for the analysis activity in an application-development life cycle.

In the third section, we then extend this simplified task model to take user group differences into consideration. We introduce a textual notation in the fourth section to record the hierarchical decomposition process of task-model construction. We also continue the case study of a personnel recruiting application by constructing a simplified task model for it.

5.1 MODELING HUMAN-COMPUTER INTERACTION

The purpose of user interface task analysis is to model the user tasks of executing computer application sessions. For many years, the GOMS model (**G**oals, **O**perators, **M**ethods, and **S**election rules) has been the subject of extensive research effort in human-computer interaction. The GOMS model is built on solid theoretical foundation and has great potential in many areas of user interface development (Card, Moran, and Newell 1983). However, it requires a well-trained, expert analyst to perform the technique; it involves a tedious analysis process; and, most important of all, it can only be conducted after a user interface is designed. Because of these concerns, the GOMS modeling technique has not been widely adopted in practice since its inception more than a decade ago. However, as we will show in the subsequent chapters, a simplified GOMS-based task model reveals abundant information to help guide the GUI application development.

In order to introduce you to the great potential of the GOMS task model, we will first review the GOMS model; then we go on to simplify it and extend it to transform it into a practical software analysis tool.

5.1.1 GOMS Task Modeling

The GOMS task model is a task-analysis approach based on a model human processor that models human behavior with three interacting subsystems: perceptual (visual and auditory perception), motor (arm-hand-finger and head-eye movement), and cognitive (decision making and memory access). These three subsystems are represented as the lowest-level operators in a GOMS model. The GOMS model can be constructed to describe the complete dynamic human-computer interaction behavior of computer users. It consists of four components: goals, operators, methods, and selection rules.

Goals. An application software is developed to help users accomplish specific goals—for example, writing a document, or designing an art work. Accomplishing a goal may take several steps. Therefore, a goal can be further decomposed into steps of subgoals. In turn, these subgoals can be further refined to finer steps, until the steps of each subgoal are all fundamental human operators. The decomposition process constructs a hierarchy of goals and their subgoals.

E X A M P L E   5 – 1

An application is developed to do a keyword search on a resume database. We can analyze the goals of a user as follows:

```
Goal: Identify job candidates.
   Goal: Specify required skills.
   Goal: Browse resumes with matching skills.
   Goal: Select candidates.
Goal: Print out candidates' resumes.
      .
      .
      .
```

As shown here, the top-level goals are decomposed into steps of subgoals.

Operators. Operators are the basic human actions that the user executes. There are three types of operators that make up fundamental human behavior:

- *Perceptual operator*—auditory and visual perception operations (e.g., listening to the warning bell, looking at on-screen information)
- *Motor operator*—arm-hand-finger and head-eye movement (e.g., pressing a key, moving a mouse)
- *Cognitive operator*—decision making, storing or retrieving an item in working memory, retrieving information from long-term memory (e.g., verifying computer display output)

Each of these operators takes some finite amount of human processing time, usually on the order of a few hundred milliseconds per operator. The total sum of these operators allows an analyst to estimate quantitatively human performance of a user interface design.

E X A M P L E   5 – 2

Continuing from the above example, we can hierarchically decompose the goals until the steps are all fundamental operators.

```
Goal: Identify job candidates.
   Goal: Specify required set of skills.
      Operator: Recall required set of skills. (Cognitive)
      Goal: Enter required set of skills.
         Operator: Type in required set of skills. (Motor)
         Goal: Verify entered data.
            Operator: Read entered data from display. (Perceptual)
            Operator: Compare with recalled skills. (Cognitive)
      .
      .
      .
```

As shown here, the decomposition process is carried out for a goal until each step is a fundamental operator.

Methods. A method is the sequence of steps that accomplishes a goal.

Depending on the level of decomposition hierarchy, the steps in a method can be subgoals, operators, or some combination of both. Much of the work in analyzing user tasks is in specifying the actual steps that users carry out in order to accomplish goals.

E X A M P L E   5 – 3

In the previous example, the steps needed to accomplish a goal make up the method for that goal.

```
Goal 1: Identify job candidates.
   Method for Goal 1:
   {
   Goal 1.1: Specify required set of skills.
      Method for Goal 1.1:
      {
      Operator 1.1.1: Recall required set of skills.
      Goal 1.1.2: Enter required set of skills.
         Method for Goal 1.1.2:
         {
         Operator 1.1.2.1: Type in required set of skills.
         Goal 1.1.2.2: Verify entered data.
            Method for Goal 1.1.2.2:
            {
            Operator 1.1.2.2.1: Read entered data from display.
            Operator 1.1.2.2.2: Compare with memorized skill set.
            }
         .
         .
         .
         }
   .
   .
   .
```

Selection Rules. There can be more than one method to accomplish a goal. A selection rule specifies certain conditions that must be satisfied before a method can be applied to accomplish a goal. If there is more than one method possible to accomplish a goal, each method would have its own steps of sub-goals and operators and an associated selection rule. A selection rule is a condition-action statement, the action being the method to be applied.

E X A M P L E   5 – 4

Still using our example, there may be several methods to accomplish the goal of identifying job candidates. One method (Method A) is to specify a set of skills and then let the application software come up with candidates possessing all the required skills. Another method (Method B) is to search using one skill at a time to gradually narrow down the pool of candidates; we would search the more important skills first.

```
Goal: Identify job candidates
   if (all required skills are equally important) then (use Method A)
   {
      .
      .
      .
      .
   }
   if (some skills are more important than others) then (use Method B)
   {
      .
      .
      .
      .
   }
```

5.2 SIMPLIFIED TASK MODEL

From the segments of the simple example we used in the last section, we can see how tedious it would be to use the same process for large applications. To construct a complete task model, an analyst would have to create a huge file. Another limiting factor is that most of the detailed information in the GOMS task model must come from a functional application, which is not practical during the analysis activity of a software development life cycle. In this section, we present a simplified task model in order to adapt it as a software analysis tool.

5.2.1 Objectives of a Simplified Task Model

As we set out to devise a simplified task-analysis process, we have several objectives in mind.

- The task model will not require any user interface design information, so we can use it during the analysis activity of a user interface software development life cycle.
- The task model will not require an analyst to be an expert cognitive psychologist. This would make it more practical for many software developers.
- The task model should be expandable to a complete GOMS task model. As a software development life cycle proceeds, a functioning prototype will become available. A full scale GOMS task model would provide valuable information for the next iteration of design improvement.

5.2.2 Simplified Task-Modeling Guidelines

Our objectives are best met by simplifying the GOMS task model. Since the hierarchy of goal decomposition in GOMS modeling represents an increasing level of detail, if we limit the task modeling to the higher-level goals and sub-goals, no design decision will be involved. The following guidelines further ensure that these objectives can be met.

- **Do the analysis top-down.** Starts the process from the most general user goal to more specific subgoals.

- **Use general terms to describe goals.** Focus on what a user would have to do to accomplish a goal, while not making any user interface design presumption in the goal statement.
- **Examine all the goals before going down to a lower level.** The breadth-first procedure considers all of the methods at one level of hierarchy before decomposing to a lower level. This allows goals and methods to be reused throughout the task model.
- **Consider all possible task scenarios to accomplish a goal.** A successful user interface design must allow users to roam freely to accomplish their tasks. Selection rules should be added to represent possible user task scenarios.
- **Use only simple sentences for the specification of goals and subgoals.** Any other sentence structure indicates that a separate goal or method should possibly be added to the task model.
- **Skip any steps of a goal that are operators.** The perceptual, motor, and cognitive operators are dependent on user interface design, which is yet to be developed.

E X A M P L E   5 – 5

```
Goal: Transfer selected text data from another application.
   Operator: Recall text data of interest.
   Goal: Locate text data to be transferred.
   Goal: Select text to be transferred from another
         application.
   Goal: Transfer selected text data to current application.
```

In this example, the steps to accomplish the goal "Transfer selected text data from another application" include a cognitive operator "Recall text data of interest". This operator step should be removed from the method.

- **Stop decomposing a goal if the steps of its methods are operators or involve user interface design presumptions.** Either of these situations signifies that we have reached the leaf nodes of the task-model hierarchy for the analysis activity.

E X A M P L E   5 – 6

```
Goal: Transfer selected text data from another application.
   Goal: Locate text data to be transferred.
   Goal: Select text data to be transferred from another
         application.
   Goal: Transfer selected text data to current application.
      Goal: Copy the selected text.
```

```
Goal: Switch focus to current application.
Goal: Position the text cursor.
Goal: Paste text at text cursor position.
```

Here, the steps to accomplish the goal "Transfer selected text data to current application" are based on the presumption that the cut-and-paste style of interapplication communication mechanism is used, which is a user interface design issue. We stop decomposing this goal any further.

5.3 Task Modeling for Multiple User-Role Applications

Among the user analysis factors presented in Chapter 4, if the user role is the dominating difference factor for the application, it would result in significantly different task models because of the different tasks to be performed for different user roles. For an application that supports a group of users assuming different roles, the top-level goals may represent some sort of organizational process flow. With all user roles involved taken into consideration, we may uncover much pertinent information that will be very useful for the subsequent life-cycle activities. It also allows us to reuse task goals and methods description and to minimize user-role-specific development effort of subsequent life-cycle activities. To consider the additional component of user roles, we need to extend the simplified task model.

The following guidelines would add the user role into our task model:

- Start specifying top-level goals with associated user roles.
- If more than one user roles share the same goal, gather these user roles under one goal.
- If all user roles share the same goal, keep only one goal statement, and remove any reference to user role.

Let's examine a personnel recruiting application as an example.

E X A M P L E   5 – 7

A personnel recruiting application supports various users involved in the personnel recruiting process. There are the recruiter from the personnel department, the hiring manager, and other hiring committee members (e.g., staff members, and other colleagues who will work closely with the person to be hired). Personnel recruiting is a process of screening a pool of job applicants to find the right match with the job requirements. The whole process may include the following top-level goals (user roles are italicized in the statements of the top level goals):

```
Goal: The hiring manager requests to fill a job opening.
Goal: The recruiter provides resumes of prospective candidates.
Goal: The hiring manager selects interview candidates.
Goal: The recruiter schedules interviews.
Goal: The interviewers provide their assessment.
```

Goal: *The hiring manager* makes a decision on the best match.
Goal: *The hiring manager* extends an offer.
Goal: *The recruiter* closes the job opening after the offer is accepted.

5.4 A TEXTUAL NOTATION FOR TASK MODELING

Although we have simplified the task model, it is still a lengthy document to produce. The development effort for the goal decomposition process, method description, and selection rules definition grows with the size and complexity of an application. In this section, we introduce a simple textual notation to allow systematic description of complex task models. The task-model notation includes elements presented in the following sections along with their associated guidelines.

5.4.1 User Roles

For an application that supports multiple user roles, the following guidelines are used to document the task model:

- Distinct user roles are denoted with the symbol **UR** followed by a number to indicate different user roles.

E X A M P L E   5 – 8

Hiring manager (UR1), personnel recruiter (UR2), other hiring committee members (UR3)

- Definition of user roles is the first part of user task-model description. A brief textual description can be attached when a user role is initially defined.

E X A M P L E   5 – 9

Hiring manager (UR1): A department manager who needs to fill an open position.

- A semicolon (;) follows the role specification to separate the roles from the remainder of task-model notation.

E X A M P L E   5 – 1 0

A goal statement specific to the hiring manager:
UR1; ...

- In the body of the task-model description, if a goal is used for more than one user role, a comma (,) separates them.

EXAMPLE 5 – 1 1

A goal statement applicable to both the hiring manager (UR1) and the recruiter (UR2):

UR1, UR2; ...

- An asterisk (*) is used if a goal statement is used by all user roles.

EXAMPLE 5 – 1 2

A goal statement applicable to all user roles:

*; ...

5.4.2 Goal Statements

Each step in a method is numbered in sequential order, and each level of decomposition is separated by a period (.). The goal numbering itself is delimited with a colon (:) and proper indentation, both of which reinforce the notion of hierarchical decomposition.

EXAMPLE 5 – 1 3

The goal of a personnel recruiter browsing resumes at some level in the decomposition is denoted as:

UR2; 2.1:   Browse resumes.

A comment starts with two slashes (//) and ends at the end of line.

EXAMPLE 5 – 1 4

```
// Browsing through resumes to examine applicants' relevant
// skill, years of experience, and so on.
UR2; 2.1:       Browse resumes.
```

5.4.3 Methods and Selection Rules

If a goal can be accomplished by using more than one method, an alphabetically ordered symbol starting with letter A would follow the sequence number for the current goal.

EXAMPLE 5 – 1 5

```
UR2; 2:  Provide resumes of prospective candidates. (Goal)
UR2; 2A: ...(Method A)
UR2; 2B: ...(Method B)
```

We describe a selection rule and the associated method as a condition-action pair. This pair follows the numbering notation. The action statement is a brief description of the method itself.

EXAMPLE 5-16

```
    UR2; 2A: if (request is urgent)
             then (search resumes on file)
```

Like goal statements, a comment starts with the characters (//) and ends at the end of line.

EXAMPLE 5-17

```
// Search resumes on file to find any prospective candidates to
// shorten the recruiting process.
UR2;2A: if (request is urgent)
        then (search resumes on file)
```

5.4.4   Reusing Goal Statements

One important purpose of the notations introduced in this section is to allow goals to be reused. To reuse a goal, simply use the same numbering label for the preexisting goal occurrence. Make sure the user roles are consistent with current context. The numbering sequence for other goals in the method still takes into account the reused goal.

EXAMPLE 5-18

```
UR2; 2.1:      Browse resume. (Preexisting Goal)
.
.
.
UR1, UR3; 3: Select candidates from a list of applicants.
UR1, UR3; 3.1: Obtain candidates' resumes.
UR1, UR3; 2.1: Browse resumes. (Goal Reused)
UR1, UR3; 3.3: Mark selected candidates. (Sequence Remains)
```

5.4.5   Additional Guidelines

As each goal has associated user roles and goal sequence numbering, the analysis document can look cluttered quickly during task modeling. For a large application, the task model produced may be difficult to follow. The following guidelines will help us avoid producing a cluttered task model.

• Enclose all the steps of a method inside {} signs to indicate a method block.

EXAMPLE 5-19

```
UR2; 2: Provide resumes of prospective candidates.
UR2; 2A: ... // A condition-action statement
```

```
{
// The steps of method A
.
.
.
}
```

- In a single-user role application, there is no need to include the user role in specifying a goal.
- Within one decomposition level where the goals all have the same numbering prefix, only current-level sequence numbering is necessary.
- The guideline above also applies to the notation for user roles, including the cases where a goal is reused.
- To reuse a preexisting goal requires the full numbering label of this goal.

EXAMPLE 5 – 20

```
UR1, UR3; 3: Select candidates from personnel-provided list.
      1:       Obtain a list of resumes from personnel.
    2.1:       Browse resumes.
      3:       Commenting on the resumes.
```

5.5   CASE STUDY: A PERSONNEL RECRUITING APPLICATION

Continue examining our case study of a personnel recruiting application, we have identified three user roles involved in this application—the hiring manager, the personnel recruiter, and other hiring committee members. The following is the task model for this application.

```
UR1: hiring manager
UR2: recruiter
UR3: other hiring committee members

UR1;1: The hiring manager requests to fill an opening.
  1.1: Specify opening requirements.
  1.2: Appoints hiring committee members.
  1.3: Send opening request to recruiter.
UR2;2: The recruiter provides resumes of prospective can-
         didates.
  2.1:  Get resumes from applicants.
  2.1A: if (request is urgent) then (use resumes on file).
  2.1B: if (job skills may be available inside) then (use
         job posting)
  2.1C: if (A and B are not sufficient) then (advertise in
         newspaper)
  2.2: Identify candidates.
    2.2.1: Enter requirements.
```

```
2.2.2: Search for applicants.
2.2.2A: if (all requirements are important)
        then (use compound search)
2.2.2B: if (some requirements are more important)
        then (use simple search)
2.2.3: Browse applicants' resumes.
2.2.4: Select candidates.
2.4: Forward resumes to the hiring manager.
UR1;3: The hiring manager selects interviewees.
3.1: Identify interviewees.
3.1.1: Browse applicants' resume.
3.1.2: Select interviewees.
3.2: Send the list of interviewees to recruiter.
UR2;4: The recruiter schedules interviews.
4.1: Find open schedule of interviewers and interviewees.
4.2: Confirm schedule with all parties.
UR3;5: The interviewers provide their assessment.
5.1: Assess candidates.
5.2: Send assessment to hiring manager and recruiter.
UR1;6: The hiring manager makes a decision on the best
       match.
6.1: Review assessments.
6.2: Decide on the best match.
UR1;7: The hiring manager extends an offer.
7.1: Inform recruiter of offer intent.
7.2: Prepare job offer.
7.3: Send out offer to recruiter and new hire.
UR2;8: The recruiter closes the job opening after the
       offer is accepted.
```

5.6 SUMMARY

In this chapter, we reviewed the GOMS task model, and later simplified it for use as a tool during the analysis activity of the development life cycle. We further extended the simplified task model to handle applications that support multiple user roles. The textual notation was also introduced to document the task model. The real-life application of an integrated recruiting application demonstrates much of the material covered in this chapter.

In Chapter 6, the task model we constructed here will guide the life-cycle activity of object-oriented analysis. As we proceed to design activities in Part 3 of this book, the task model will be constantly referenced. With the GOMS model as the basis of our simplified task model, the benefits of our task model go beyond the life-cycle activities we cover in this book, especially the evaluation and redesign iterations of user interface design.

5.7 BIBLIOGRAPHIC NOTES

The best reference of the original GOMS task analysis is the book written by the pioneers of this approach as well as many other advances in human-computer interaction (Card, Moran, and Newell 1983), which also offers extensive information on the cognitive psychology aspects of human-computer interaction. Subsequent research has extended the model to apply it to various aspects of user interface development (Kieras 1988, 1991; Bovair, Kieras, and Polson 1990; Elkerton 1988; Gong and Elkerton 1990; John 1988, 1990; John, Vera, and Newell 1990).

Some of this work has helped promote GOMS task analysis as a viable quantitative tool for engineering human-computer interfaces (Kieras 1988, 1991; Bovair, Kieras, and Polson 1990). In other research (Elkerton 1988; Gong and Elkerton 1990), the GOMS task analysis is applied to the development of on-line help system and documentation for human-computer interfaces, which shows the versatility of GOMS task-analysis app roach in addressing many practical issues of human-computer interfaces.

The GOMS model has been extended to study human-computer interaction of highly interactive and dynamic audio-visual systems (John 1988, 1990; John, Vera, and Newell 1990). In our opinion, these researchers made a significant contribution toward practical GOMS task analysis by introducing the schedule chart representation used in project management application to represent the GOMS task model.

Although we simplified the GOMS task model to adapt it for the analysis activity of GUI application development, the potential value of a fully expanded GOMS task model is enormous in many other aspects of GUI development, as suggested by these cited references.

Constructing an Object Model

To continue the analysis activity of the GUI application-development life cycle, we present a procedure for constructing a user interface-level object model from the user task model introduced in the previous chapter.

We first discuss a user interface-level object model, which differs from other software-level object models because of its user perspective. The user interface-level object model has many of the same elements as a software-level object model, with the addition of attribute facets and alternative views to improve user task performance.

We then present a procedure to construct a user interface-level object model from the task model. Although the user interface-level object model shares many elements with a software-level object model, we identify these elements with criteria derived from user perspectives.

Finally, there is a notation for the object-model elements of attribute facets and alternative views to supplement the object model notation of other popular object-oriented software development approaches. We also continue the case study of a personnel recruiting application by constructing a user interface-level object model for it.

6.1 OBJECT MODEL

The object-oriented approach has evolved over the years to address many critical concerns in software development, such as software reuse and software maintenance. A number of object-modeling approaches have been developed from the perspective of software-system developers. For example, well-known approaches have been developed for software-system development in general (Booch 1991; Rumbaugh et al. 1991; Shlaer and Mellor 1988, 1992; Coad and Yourdon 1991).

However, when we are developing GUI applications, our first priority is to address the needs of users. Although the software-level object model does benefit the implementation effort of GUI software systems, it falls short of doubling as a user interface-level object model.

In the following subsection, we discuss a user interface-level object model tailored to the needs of users, as well as a procedure to construct a user interface-level object model from the user task model.

6.1.1 User Interface-Level Object Model

A user interface object model must meet the objective of helping users perform their tasks. In object-oriented GUIs, users interact with application objects, which are also the focus of attention throughout users' application task-performing sessions. A user interface-level object model must provide extensive application object information and easy access to it, while allowing the user to focus on specific aspects of object information. Users shouldn't have to recall detailed information from memory or mentally derive critical information in their application sessions.

A user interface-level object model has the elements of objects, relationships among objects, attributes of an object, operations of an attribute, facets of an attribute, and alternative views of an object. Objects can also be further abstracted into individual classes or grouped into aggregation or container classes. There may also be inheritance relationships among classes due to various considerations in specialization or generalization.

Objects. The application objects of a user interface application are the focus of attention throughout users' task-performing sessions. Depending on the application, there may be several application objects, some of which are primary and others are secondary. In this chapter, we will focus on identifying these objects, not on their relative importance in an application.

Relationships Among Objects. Objects are interconnected by various relationships among them. Information flows among objects through these relationships. Users can enact information transfer among related objects.

Object Attributes. Each object is characterized by a set of attributes. When we construct a user interface-level object model, we identify attributes that directly convey object information to users. It is subtly different from a software-level object model (Shlaer and Mellor 1988), which only considers mutually independent and fully factored attributes.[*]

Object Operations. Operations of an object perform certain actions on the object attributes. Users select an operation to access the attributes of an object, change to an alternative view, or change the values of attributes.

Attribute Facets. An attribute is further characterized by its facets—possible values, default value, unit of measurement, access level, and so on. Presenting the facets of an attribute relieves users from memorizing them and helps users in setting the correct values of an attribute. This element is usually lacking in object models at the software level, but it is a critical element in the object model at the user interface level.

Alternative Views. An application object is characterized by several attributes. Depending on the user preferences or on the tasks a user is performing, alternative views of an object allow a user to focus on some subsets of object attributes of interests.

Classes. An object is an instance of a certain class. Each instance of a class has its own set of attribute values. Objects of the same class share the same attributes, operations, attribute facets, and alternative views.

Aggregation Classes. Aggregation classes contain other classes (Smith and Smith 1977; Liu 1992). For example, a document class is an aggregation class that contains a text class, a drawing class, a graph class, and so on. A drawing class is itself also an aggregation class that contains various line drawing and shape classes.

Container Classes. A container class contains object instances of the same class or those that have a common superclass. A list, a table, or a tree data structured class are examples of a container class.

Subclass/Superclass Inheritance Relationships.[**] Specialization of

---

[*] Fully factored attributes are not derivable from other attributes. For example, the perimeter and the area of a circular shape are mutually indepentent, but both are derivable from the radius of the circle, which is a fully factored attribute.

[**] Class inheritance relationships have been extensively examined in many other books on object-oriented software development appoaches. This element of a user interface-level object model is the same as a software-level object model, and we will concentrate our discussion on user interface application-specific issues.

classes' attributes or operations creates subclasses. Generalization of classes' attributes and operations creates superclasses.

6.2   USER INTERFACE-LEVEL OBJECT-MODELING PROCEDURE

In the next sections, we discuss a procedure to construct the user interface-level object model of an application from its user task model. All the elements of a user interface-level object model described in the previous section will be identified in this procedure.

In the last chapter, we discussed user task modeling. Users accomplish their tasks one step at a time. Each of these steps is a goal statement of a verb-noun pair; the verb portion states an action, and the noun portion defines the object accepting the action. By analyzing the task model, we are immediately able to identify objects and actions. Then we can construct a user interface-level object model by further identifying the elements of the relationships among objects, object attributes, object operations, attribute facets, and alternative views. We then refine the object model by grouping objects that are instances of a class or part of an aggregation or a container class. Afterward, we further abstract the classes to form a class-inheritance hierarchy.

6.2.1   Grammatical Analysis of Task-Model Statements

One of the guidelines we have presented for task modeling is to use simple-sentence goal statements. Each goal statement describes a step to accomplish a task. Analyzing the grammar of these simple sentences can help us identify elements of a user interface-level object model in the subsequent sections.

Examining the case study in Chapter 5, we see that the top-level goals of the task model are complete sentences, with subject and predicate. As the top-level goals are further decomposed into the next level of subgoals, subgoal statements are usually predicates of verb-noun pairs with an implicit subject of user role to form complete sentences as shown in Figure 6-1.

(The hiring manager)   extends an offer.
subject   predicate

Figure 6–1. Goal statements are usually predicates with user roles as the implicit subjects.

Although the sentences of task goals are usually simple sentences, their structures can take on various forms. On examining these sentences, the following grammatical patterns emerge:

- The predicates of goal statements may consist of a transitive verb and a direct object.

EXAMPLE   6 – 1

The hiring manager <u>selects</u> <u>interviewees.</u>

The double-underlined word is a transitive verb. The single-underlined phrase is the direct object.

- Occasionally a predicate includes both a direct object and an indirect object. The indirect object always precedes the direct object.

EXAMPLE   6 – 2

The recruiter sends <u>the hiring manager</u> <u>a list of candidates.</u>

The single-underlined phrase is the indirect object, and the double-underlined phrase is the direct object.

- We can reorder a predicate with an indirect object and add a preposition to change the indirect object into an object of the preposition.

EXAMPLE   6 – 3

---

*The recruiter sends <u>a list of candidates</u> **to** <u>the hiring manager.</u>*

The single-underlined noun phrase, an indirect object in the last example, becomes an object of the preposition **to**.

As the goal decomposition progresses, the task subgoals are described with predicates of simple transitive verbs and direct object pairs. The user roles are the implied subject counterpart of the predicates to make up complete sentences. We can identify the elements of user interface-level object model such as objects, relationships among objects, and object attributes from predicates of goal statements.

6.2.2 Identifying Objects

The first step in object modeling is to identify objects. In a user interface-level object model, this involves identifying objects that users interact with as they perform application tasks.

The general procedure for identifying objects from an application task model has the following steps:

1 **Extract direct and indirect objects from the predicates as candidate objects.**

The direct and indirect objects of a transitive verb in the predicates receive user actions. The subjects of the task goal-statement sentences are user roles that may not be user objects. If a user role appears as a direct or indirect object, it is a candidate application object

2 **Find hidden candidate objects.**

Not all objects are directly identifiable from an application task model; they need to be obtained from the user interface developer's and application-domain expert's knowledge. Also, task modeling may not have covered all possible user tasks. As in the case study of the personnel recruiting application in Chapter 5, the task goals of initial installation and routine application maintenance of a system administrator's role were not considered in the task model.

E X A M P L E   6 – 4

(The system administrator) changes <u>system configuration</u>.
A new candidate object of **system configuration** should be added.

---

3 Prune candidate objects.

Remove objects that should be considered as attributes instead. In task models, as subgoals are decomposed into the finer detail of steps, the direct objects in the predicates may become attributes of an object. Although the object attributes should also be identified, they should be excluded here so that we retain only the objects. It is also possible that we will find an attribute that would be more appropriately modeled as an object after several iterations of object modeling.

E X A M P L E   6 – 5

Specify the <u>salary</u>.
The salary may have been identified as an object initially, but, on closer examination, the salary can be an attribute of a **job-offer** object.

6.2.3   Identifying Relationships

The application objects we identified in the last section are not isolated islands; they are interconnected and interact with each other. In object-oriented approaches, these links are instances of an association class (Rumbaugh et al. 1991). From a task model, we can identify many dynamic relationships among objects. There are also other structural relationships among objects to be identified from the application domain knowledge.

Dynamic Relationships. As shown in the grammatical analysis section, the predicates of task model statement can contain both a direct object and an indirect object. We can rewrite these predicates to turn the indirect object into the object of an added preposition. The preposition relates the direct object of the transitive verb and the object of the preposition. In short, the direct object and the indirect object are related.

E X A M P L E   6 – 6

The recruiter sends <u>the hiring manager</u> <u>a list of candidates.</u>

*The recruiter sends <u>a list of candidates</u> **to** <u>the hiring manager.</u>*

<u>A list of candidates</u> is sent to <u>the hiring manager</u> by the recruiter.

The three sentences are equivalent, with relationship between the single-underlined application object, **the hiring manager**, and the double-underlined application object, **a list of candidates**.

These examples provide the following guideline in identifying relationships among application objects from a task model:

In a predicate that contains both a direct and an indirect object, the direct object and the indirect object are related. The transitive verb also defines the relationship.

Other Structural Relationships. Although dynamic relationships imply underlying structural relationships, there are many other structural relationships among the objects that are not explicitly stated in the task model as dynamic relationships and that have to be identified from application domain knowledge. A common structural relationship in real-world applications is the aggregation relationship (also known as has-a or part-of relationships) among objects in an object model.

E X A M P L E   6 – 7

An applicant **has a** resume.
The hiring manager's schedule **includes** interview appointments.

Relationship Multiplicity. Multiplicity is the number of class instances that may have to do with a related class instance. Depending on the application, the relationships can be one-to-one, one-to-many, or many-to-many.

E X A M P L E   6 – 8

one-to-one:	(The hiring manager) **sends** opening request to the recruiter.
one-to-many:	(The recruiter) **sends** resumes to hiring committee members.
many-to-many:	The interviewers **send** their assessments to the recruiter and the hiring manager.

Relationship Directionality. Structural relationships are generally bidirectional. A dynamic relationship specifies directional action, but it can be modeled as an instance of a more general bidirectional association class.

E X A M P L E   6 – 9

In the task goal statement

*The hiring manager **sends** the opening request **to** the recruiter.*

the single-directional dynamic relationship ***sends to*** may be an instance of a more general bidirectional association class ***communicate with.***

6.2.4 Identifying Attributes

A set of attributes characterizes an object. We do not usually explicitly state the attributes of an object in our task model because it is quite time-consuming to generate such a large amount of detailed information. The attributes are most likely obtained from the knowledge of domain experts and experienced application developers. After the initial attributes are acquired, we can prune or expand them by applying the following guidelines.

Keep Only the Relevant Set. Although an application object can have a number of inherent characteristics, we keep only the ones that are specific to the application of interest.

E X A M P L E   6 – 1 0

A paragraph object in a desktop publishing application may have the attributes of

font type

font size

line spacing

indentation

alignment

But in a writing-style analysis application, the same paragraph object is better characterized by the grammatical attributes of its sentences, such as

the purpose of a sentence (declarative, interrogative, imperative, or exclamatory)

the internal structure of a sentence (simple, compound, complex, or compound complex).

Keep Alternative Sets of Attributes. In a user interface-level object model, we can present an object and its attributes in alternative views to adapt to user preferences. One form of alternative view is to represent the object with an alternative set of attributes. Alternative sets of attributes are mutually dependent and transformable from one to the other.

E X A M P L E   6 – 1 1

A **color** object has the attributes of

color name (brown, red, aqua marine, and so on)

color model (RGB, HSV, and so on)

color component values

or is alternatively represented with the attributes of

color name

colormap file name

colormap entry index value, and so on.

In the two alternative representations of this example, color-component values can be interchangeably transformed into other color-model values; a specific colormap entry also corresponds to a color model representation. As we will discuss further in a later section on identifying alternative views, we identify these sets of mutually dependent attributes in order to present alternative views of an application object according to user preferences.

Identify Essential Derivable Attributes. Our objective in identifying object attributes is to satisfy user needs. Contrary to recommendations of other object-oriented software-analysis approaches, we identify as many derivable attributes as necessary in order to save users from having to derive them manually during their application sessions. Derivable attributes are usually read-only.

E X A M P L E   6 – 1 2

A **rectangle** object has the attributes of:

width

height

area

The area attribute is derivable from the width and height attributes.

E X A M P L E   6 – 1 3

A **stock transaction** object in a stock-trading application may have the attributes of:

current price

daily high

daily low

The *daily high* and *daily low* price levels are derived from current price history of the day.

6.2.5 Identifying Facets of Each Attribute

Facets[*] are the properties of an attribute that we use to describe the characteristics of the attribute. The facets of an attribute may include access level, current value, default value, possible values, alternative representations, and so on. The default value and possible values relieve users from memorizing detailed information and prevent them from making mistakes.

Assigning Default Attribute Values. An attribute has changing values to reflect the current state of an object. In user interface applications, values of attributes change as a result of user actions or application's internal state changes. However, when an object is initialized, default attribute values are assigned to object attributes.

Identifying Possible Attribute Values. In user interface applications, an object attribute may have a limited range of possible values. For an operation that changes the value of an attribute, GUI design often presents the attribute's possible values to allow user selection by direct manipulation, which helps improve user performance while preventing user errors.

E X A M P L E   6 – 1 4

In the personnel recruiting application, the **interview schedule** object has the attributes:

time of day:	from 8:30 A.M.–5:30 P.M., in 15-minute increments.
date:	any weekday during the following two weeks.
duration:	30–60 minutes, in 15-minute increments.

Identifying Alternative Attribute Representation. We can represent an attribute or a set of attributes in several ways (e.g., in different units). Depending on a user's preference, he or she might select one representation over the others.

E X A M P L E   6 – 1 5

The *position* attribute of an object in a plane-geometry application:

rectangular coordinates: x, y

polar coordinates: r, α

The *temperature* attribute of an object in a weather-forecasting application:

Celsius: 10 degrees

Fahrenheit: 50 degrees

---

[*] In knowledge representation, frames contain slots and slots contain facets, which is analogous to objects having attributes and attributes having facets.

6.2.6 Identifying Alternative Views

In GUI design, we can represent application objects and their attributes in different ways to suit individual users' preferences. The alternative views of an object may include the following cases:

An Alternative Application Metaphor of an Object. To understand a metaphor, the user needs to have the prior experience of it. Depending on users' own experiences, they may prefer that an application object be represented in certain metaphor.

E X A M P L E   6 – 1 6

A **file** object:
file cabinet metaphor:	*files = > file folders in a file cabinet*
tree-structure metaphor:	*files = > leaf nodes in a tree data structure*

An Alternative Representation of an Object. We can represent an object in a different scale or a different set of attributes. Depending on the context and a user's preferences, a representation may be selected by a user. Earlier in this chapter, we presented an example of a color object that can be represented in alternative sets of attributes.

A Selective Subset of an Object's Attributes. An object can have a number of attributes. If represented simultaneously, they may appear cluttered and be difficult to differentiate. The user may also want to concentrate on certain aspects of an object, while ignoring other attributes.

E X A M P L E   6 – 1 7

A **file** object has the following attributes:

file name—always important to a user

file size—useful when a user is concerned about disk space a file takes

file type—useful when a user wants to narrow the search to text file only

date of last modification—useful when a user wants to find an updated file

A Different Ordering of the Members of a Container Object. The member objects of a container object can be displayed in various sorting orders based on different attributes.

E X A M P L E   6 – 1 8

A **file directory** is a container object that contains **file** member objects. The directory can be displayed by sorting its member objects with their file name, file size, or date of last modification.

6.2.7 Identifying Operations

The operations of an application object are the user actions that change current state, inquire current state, or select alternative views. An operation changes the state of an object by changing the values of its attributes. Most operations change the value of writable attributes or query the current value of a readable attribute.

Commonly provided operations such as the *create* and *delete* operations allow users to control the life cycle of an application object. The operations of *find, cut, copy,* and *paste* allow users to edit application objects. There are also the operations that we would put under the category of alternative views, such as zoom, and sort by an attribute.

6.2.8 Identifying Classes

Each object is an instance of a certain class. We can characterize objects of the same class by the same set of alternative views, attributes, and operations, although their attributes' values may vary with each instance. By grouping objects that have the same set of object elements into classes of objects, we improve the abstraction and reusability of an object model.

E X A M P L E   6 – 1 9

In the personnel recruiting application, user accounts are instances of a **user account class**, which has the following elements:

Attributes: Name, account name, password, and so on.

Operations: Change name, account name, password; create account; delete account.

Each user account has its own name, account name, and password. Each user account is also involved in some job opening cases, which are instances of an **opening-case** class. The operations of this class can change attribute values and create and delete an account.

6.2.9 Identifying Aggregation and Container Classes

An aggregation class (also known as compound class or composite class) is composed of other classes. An aggregation class also has its own relationships, attributes, operations, and alternative views.

E X A M P L E   6 – 2 0

A document class is an aggregation class that is composed of a drawing class, a graph class, a text class, and so on.

A container class contains object instances of one class. Container classes are often implemented as tree, list, table, or array data structures.

E X A M P L E   6 – 2 1

A **candidate-list** object is an instance of a container class that contains a list of **candidate** objects.

6.2.10 Identifying Class Inheritance Relationships

Although up to this point we have been concerned only with concrete classes[*] in a user interface-level object model, inheritance relationships can exist among these concrete classes.

Class inheritance hierarchy consists of superclasses and subclasses. A superclass is a generalization of the subclasses that share some common characteristics of the superclass (i.e., attributes, operations, and alternative views). A subclass is a specialization or restriction of its superclass. The specialization process may involve adding (or overriding) alternative views, operations, or attributes to a class to produce a new subclass.

E X A M P L E   6 – 2 2

An **applicant** class is the superclass of a **candidate** class, which in turn is the superclass of an **interviewee** class. As each subclass is the result of screening from its superclass, the subclass has additional attributes and operations.

6.3 Notation for User Interface-Level Object Model

In this chapter, we have presented a user interface-level object model with the elements of objects, relationships among objects, attributes, operations, alternative views of an object, and attribute facets. Objects can be grouped further into classes. Some classes are also identified as aggregation classes, which contain other classes.

This process of object modeling is evolutionary and iterative in practice. As we present additional development activities in subsequent chapters, the object model will be improved incrementally to reflect the priority of object-model elements and then mapped with a user interface metaphor.

Almost every object-oriented software approach offers some type of notation to represent the object model. Looking at its composition, the user interface-level object model differs from software-level object model by having two additional elements: the attribute facets and the alternative views. We can adopt an existing software-level object-model notation by supplementing it with notations for attribute facets and alternative views.

---

[*] A concrete class can have object instances, as opposed to an abstract class that cannot have object instances.

6.3.1   Notation for Attribute Facets

Attribute facets are an added level of information in the user interface-level object model. Each object attribute may have a different set of facets, analogous to a class characterized by a set of attributes. Therefore, we can use a notation similar to a class to represent the facets of an attribute (see Figure 6-2).

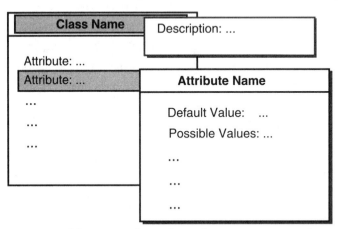

Figure 6–2.   Notation of attribute facets represented as the next level of class notation.

6.3.2   Notation for Alternative Views

The alternative views of a class present its alternative visual representations. Alternative views are listed with the attributes and operations in a class notation (see Figure 6-3). Each alternative view must have a detailed description of its features.

6.4   CASE STUDY: A PERSONNEL RECRUITING APPLICATION

In the case study we've been using in previous chapters, we have analyzed the personnel recruiting application. In this section, we continue studying this application by constructing a user interface-level object model for it.

6.4.1   Identifying Objects

First we will go through the task model we constructed in the last chapter to identify objects from task goal statements. There are other objects that are also necessary for the application, such as the system administrator and user accounts. We found the following objects:

job-opening request, job requirement, job applicants, job candidates, job interviewees, new hire, job offer, resume, interview schedule, interview assessment,

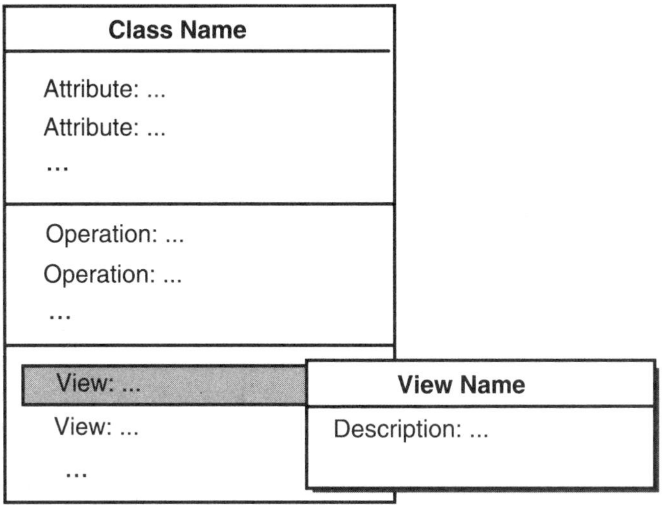

Figure 6–3.   The alternative views are listed together with the attributes and operations of a class.

hiring manager, personnel recruiter, hiring committee, hiring committee members, system administrator, user accounts, job-opening case.

6.4.2   Identifying Other Object-Model Elements

For each of the objects identified, we also identify the relationships, operations, attributes, and alternative views of these objects (see Table 6-1).

The objects and their dynamic relationships are depicted in Figure 6-4. In Figure 6-5, we also show the objects and their aggregation relationships.

6.4.3   Grouping Objects into Classes

Examining the objects we have identified, we can see that each one of them can be a standalone class. There is no need to group them further into classes.

6.4.4   Identifying Aggregation Classes and Container Classes

Looking through the identified classes, we find several classes are aggregation classes as shown in Figure 6-5. There are also a number of container classes, such as the list of applicants, list of candidates, and list of interviewees (see Figure 6-6).

6.4.5   Identifying Class Inheritance Relationships

We can further analyze the object model to identify inheritance relationships among the classes. The superclass/subclass relationships exist among a number of the classes. For example, the **job-candidate** class is a specialization of the **job-applicant** class because of additional criteria that are met by an

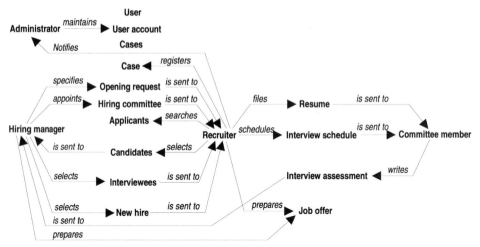

Figure 6–4.   Objects and the dynamic relationships among them.

Table 6–1 Object Model of the Personnel Recruiting Application

Object	Relationship	Operation	Attribute	Facet	Alternative View
opening request	1. has requirements 2. is sent to recruiter	1. open 2. close 3. browse 4. create 5. edit 6. delete	1. title 2. priority 3. hiring manager 4. job responsibility	1. job titles in a department 2. low/ medium/ high 3. all managers 4. Textual statements	1. A view containing all attributes 2. A view using the *forms* metaphor
job applicant	1. has resume 2. applies for an opening	1. create 2. select 3. delete	1. name 2. status 3. availability	1. (from resume file) 2. candidate/to be interviewed/ interviewed 3. date	1. name attribute view 2. name and status view 3. name, status, and availability view
.					
.					
.					

applicant to qualify as a job candidate. In Figure 6-7, we show the additional inheritance relationships among the classes. The user interface-level object model is thus fully constructed. In the following chapters, when we present GUI design activities, we will refine this object model further.

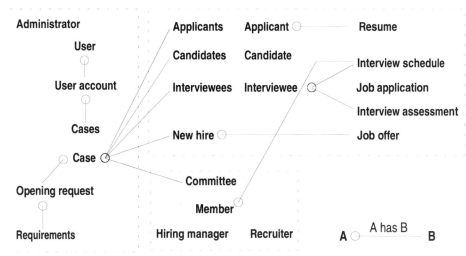

Figure 6–5. Objects and the aggregation relationships among them.

Figure 6–6. The container classes in the object world.

6.5 SUMMARY

The object model we have presented in this chapter is at the user interface-level, which differs from the software-level object model described in many popular references on object-oriented software development approaches (see cited references in the next section). As we continue in the following chapters, we will refine the object model to reflect the priority of each class, relationship,

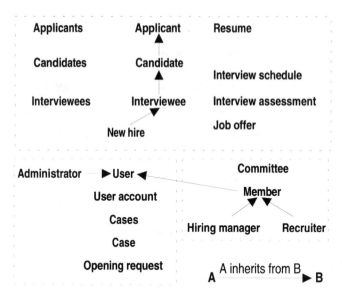

Figure 6–7.   The inheritance relationships among classes.

attribute, and operation. In Chapter 8, we will devise a user interface metaphor to map this object model. Then in Chapter 9, we will be able to map this high-level abstracted object model into a GUI design conforming to any user interface style guide.

We can further abstract the user interface-level object model to transform it into a software-level object model by generalizing classes into superclasses. This improves software reusability and extendibility further by introducing inheritance into the object model. Although we have focused our presentation on the user interface-level object model with concrete classes in this chapter, there may very well exist inheritance relationships among the concrete classes. It is significant that our approach is versatile in handling various concerns of GUI application development, from user task performance, user interface style specific design, and user interface metaphor design to object-oriented software implementation.

6.6   BIBLIOGRAPHIC NOTES

The object-oriented software development approaches introduced recently (Shlaer and Mellor 1988, 1992; Wirfs-Brock, Wilkerson, and Wiener 1990; Booch 1991; Coad and Yourdon 1991; Rumbaugh et al. 1991) have addressed software development concerns in general. Although our development approach is specifically intended for GUI applications, we have followed the same terminology used in these object-oriented software development approaches. We can go beyond the user interface-level object model to construct the software-level object model.

Although task scenarios has been introduced for dynamic modeling of system behavior (Rumbaugh et al. 1991), the object model was constructed with only information from the problem statement. We instead have constructed the user interface-level object model from the task model introduced in the previous chapter, which is more structured and comprehensive in revealing user task-performing information and which can also be used for dynamic modeling.

Walk-through has also been used to construct an object model (Wirfs-Brock, Wilkerson, and Wiener 1990). Although walk-through reveals more information than a problem statement, it is not as structured as a task model, which is also extendible to a complete GOMS task model for the evaluation of a user interface design.

Readers can find extensive evaluation and comparison of all the object-oriented software development approaches mentioned here (Arnold et al. 1991; de Champeaux 1991). The strength of our approach is mainly in the development of user interface applications. We expect readers to adopt one or more of these software approaches to complement our approach in other software development issues, such as class-inheritance abstraction, system-dynamic behavior, and process functions.

GRAPHICAL USER INTERFACE DESIGN ACTIVITIES

User Interface System-Level Design

*I*n this chapter, we present the system-level design activity of GUIs. In applications that have dominating difference factors, users perform different tasks depending on which user group they belong to, while interacting with a specific set of application objects. We begin this chapter by discussing system partitioning of a user interface-level object model based on the dominating difference factor of user groups, where application objects for each user group are identified.

Once we have partitioned a user interface-level object model, we continue with system-level design by revisiting the task model we constructed in Chapter 5. The task model contains information of the dynamic behavior of user interaction with application objects. From this we can determine the priority of application objects, relationships, attributes, operations, and alternative views in the user-group-partitioned user interface-level object model. Grouping object-model elements into small logical groups is also necessary to further control the complexity of a GUI and to improve user performance.

We then address the design issue of error-recovery behavior. Since the task model was constructed with the unrealistic assumption of error-free task performance, we first examine the task model to find possible error scenarios, and then we present common user interface design practices that can prevent users from making errors and help them to recover from error states.

7.1 SYSTEM PARTITIONING ON USER-GROUP BOUNDARIES

For each specific application, the result of user analysis may reveal different dominating difference factors. For example, the dominating difference factor for a computer game software may be the application-domain skill-level difference. The same approach we present in this chapter for user-role difference factors can be equally applied to any other dominating user difference factors that would result in distinct user groups.

In the case study we have been using in previous chapters, the user role has been a determining factor in user analysis. In Chapter 5, we presented a task model considering user-role differences, which describes the different tasks performed by different user roles. The user-role difference was also reflected in the user interface-level object model we constructed in Chapter 6, with each user role interacting with a subset of classes.

In this section, as we begin the discussion of user interface design activities, we first explain our rationale for partitioning the object model. Then we explicitly partition the user interface-level object model based on different user roles. This leads to the subsequent user interface design activities that accommodate the needs of distinct user groups.

7.1.1 Rationale of Object-Model Partitioning

When the user role is the dominating difference factor in user analysis, user-role differences may result in many different specialization of classes in a user interface-level object model. The rationale for partitioning the user interface-level object model based on user roles includes:

- Different user roles interact with a specific subset of classes in a user interface-level object model. A partitioned object model helps us to focus on the dominating difference factor.
- Although different user roles may access different classes that have a common superclass, these classes would share some common dynamic relationships, attributes, operations, and alternative views. Any specialization or restriction in a subclass cannot be shared among the sibling subclasses, nor by their superclass.

EXAMPLE   7 – 1

The **interview schedule** class in the personnel recruiting application is only readable by interviewers. A specialized subclass **recruiter's interview schedule** would allow personnel recruiters to schedule an interview, and make changes if necessary. Throughout the interviewers' task performing sessions, they have no access to object instances of a **recruiter's interview schedule** class.

- Even for those classes that are shareable among different user roles, other differences in domain knowledge, computer skills, and usage pattern may still require customized user interface design for different user groups.

E X A M P L E   7 – 2

A recruiter may be handling several opening requests from a number of hiring managers simultaneously. Therefore the recruiter will be using the personnel recruiting application much more frequently than the individual hiring manager. The personnel recruiters have more extensive domain knowledge and would quickly become experienced users of the application because of their frequent usage. On the contrary, a hiring manager may require the service of personnel recruiter only occasionally and may have limited domain knowledge of the personnel recruiting process. Users from these two different groups interact with application objects in a different pattern.

To address these variation factors among user groups, we need to specialize the user interface design to accommodate their differences. Also, since we don't want to increase dramatically the overall development effort, a class shared among user groups should be carefully specialized into subclasses.

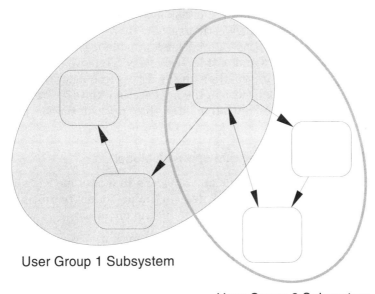

User Group 1 Subsystem

User Group 2 Subsystem

Figure 7–1. Object-model partitioning on boundaries of user groups.

7.1.2   Partitioning the User Interface-Level Object Model

Once the dominating user difference factors are identified, we can begin the system partitioning on the boundaries that separate user groups. As we have discussed in Chapter 4, distinct user groups perform their tasks differently. We should tailor GUI design to the specific needs of these distinct user groups.

Identifying a subset of classes for each user role from a user interface-level object model results in a partitioned system (see Figure 7-1). Depending on the user role, a class may have access restrictions applied (e.g., write, read-only, no access), which suggests that further specialization or restriction of classes into subclasses is necessary.

7.2   DYNAMIC BEHAVIOR IN A TASK MODEL

In object-oriented analysis activity, we have identified objects and dynamic relationships from the task-model specification. A dynamic relationship can be viewed as an external event that changes the state of an object. By including the selection rules in the task model, and the classes and dynamic relationships in the user interface-level object model, we can construct a state transition diagram. The events in this state transition diagram are dynamic relationships resulting from user actions. A state transition diagram provides valuable information for software design. The focus in user interface system-level design is to prioritize the elements of the user interface-level object model.

In this section, we first examine the task goal statements in the task model to identify user-initiated events. We then group these events with the corresponding classes into object-action pairs. These provide the information of task execution order among classes and within each class. Then we enumerate possible task scenarios to provide information on the access frequency of the elements of an object model. As we will discuss in the next section, the execution order and access pattern (frequency and duration) are the two criteria for prioritizing object-model elements.

7.2.1   Event Sequence Diagram of a Task Model

We can represent the task goals and subgoals in a task model as events in an event sequence diagram. Figure 7-2 depicts the personnel recruiting application example with notations that have the following meaning:

- Each column contains the sequence of events for a user role.
- A solid horizontal line indicates an action being applied to another user role. The receiver of such an action has an arrowhead on its column boundary.
- Events have dotted underlines if they are user actions that are done offline. We use them in the diagram to preserve the continuity of event sequences.

We collect the events into the more compact event list shown in Figure 7-3.

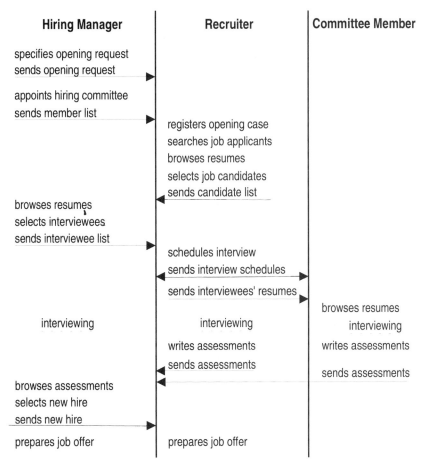

Figure 7–2.   Event sequence diagram constructed from a task model.

7.2.2   Sequences of Object-Action Pairs

Each event in the event list is an object-action pair. During object-oriented analysis activity, we have identified objects and actions and constructed a user interface-level object model from them. This information will be used in the software design of application functional core and subsequent GUI design activities. We show the object-action pairs for each user role in Figure 7-4, where the actions are either operations or dynamic relationships of an object.

7.2.3   Enumerating Task Scenarios

A task scenario is a task-execution path that goes through the steps and decomposition levels of task goals. By enumerating possible task scenarios, we

Hiring Manager	Recruiter	Committee Member
specifies opening request	registers opening case	browses resumes
sends opening request	searches job applicants	writes assessments
appoints hiring committee	browses resumes	sends assessments
sends member list	selects job candidates	
browses resumes	sends candidate list	
selects interviewees	schedules interviews	
sends interviewee list	sends interview schedules	
browses assessments	sends interviewees' resumes	
selects new hire	writes interview assessments	
sends new hire	sends assessments	
prepares job offer	prepares job offer	

Figure 7–3. Event list for each user role.

can estimate the access frequency and duration of object-model elements in users' task-performing sessions. The event sequences and object-action pairs we have derived in the previous sections help us to focus on the object-model elements, rather than the individual task goal statements of a task model.

Without more reliable statistics gathered from actual user usability testing or computer simulation, the enumeration of task scenarios and the access-pattern estimation are highly dependent on developers' experience and application domain knowledge.

7.3 PRIORITIZING OBJECT-MODEL ELEMENTS

A user of a specific user role interacts with a set of application objects. Depending on the order of execution and the frequency of execution, we can establish the priority of these application objects and their object elements (dynamic relationships, attributes, operations, and so on). In Chapter 8, we will use the information of class priority to find a source metaphor that best represents the target application. The priority of an application class also determines whether it will be presented as the primary or the secondary window in object-oriented GUI design and will be discussed in Chapter 9.

Depending on a specific user role, the instances of classes are accessed in a certain execution order and at different frequency/duration. Prioritizing and grouping object-model elements will allow us to organize them into several windows, which are displayed in a certain sequence in response to user interaction.

7.3.1 Identifying Concurrent Application Objects

Throughout a user's task-execution path, relevant application objects need

Hiring Manager		Recruiter		Committee Members	
Objects	Actions	Objects	Actions	Objects	Actions
Opening request	create edit send delete	Opening request	browse	Interview schedule	browse
		Opening case	create edit delete	Resume	browse
Hiring committee	create edit send delete	Applicant list	create edit	Assessment	create edit send delete
Resume	browse	Resume	browse send create delete		
Candidate list	browse				
interviewee list	create edit send delete	Candidate list	create edit send delete		
Interview schedule	browse	interviewee list	browse		
Assessment	browse	Interview schedule	create edit send delete		
New hire	create edit send delete				
		Assessment	create edit send delete		
Job offer	create edit send delete	Job offer	edit		

Figure 7–4. Objects and their respective actions for each user role.

to be presented to provide context-sensitive information. A user's access level of application objects in a particular context may vary, but the user should be allowed to access several application objects simultaneously to perform tasks. In the following example scenarios, a user will need concurrent presentation of some subset of application objects.

E X A M P L E   7 – 3

1 The recruiter searches through the resumes to find candidates that match the opening request of the hiring manager.

To perform the task goal of searching resumes, the recruiter needs access to both the resume objects and the opening request object. The searching process is guided by the requirements stated in the opening request. Two application objects (the **resume** and the **opening request**) may need to be presented simultaneously.

2 *The hiring manager forwards candidates' resumes to hiring committee members.*
To perform the task goal of forwarding candidates' resumes, the hiring manager identifies the staff members in his organization that will interact with the person to be hired. The hiring manager may want to attach the **opening request** object to the resumes to inform the hiring committee members. The hiring manager may need the organization chart to identify the staff member that should be involved in the hiring process. Three application objects (the **opening request**, the **resume**, and the **organization chart**) may need to be presented simultaneously.

3 *A hiring committee member writes down comments after interviewing a candidate.*
Any comment on a candidate should be based on the requirements of the opening, the candidate's resume, and the interview itself. Three application objects (the **opening request**, the **resume**, and the **interview assessment**) may be needed simultaneously by a user of the hiring-committee-member user role.

7.3.2   Prioritizing Application Objects

In a typical GUI application, a number of application objects may be involved. To help the users focus on the relevant application objects to perform their tasks, and to better use the limited screen-display real estate, we need to prioritize the application objects in order to determine the sequence of application-object presentation.

The priority of an application object is based on two criteria: the access frequency/duration and the execution order.

Access Frequency/Duration. In a user's application session, we should treat the most frequently used application objects as the primary focus of a GUI application. As the primary focus, an application object should remain on screen to allow ready access by the user.

E X A M P L E   7 – 4

1 For the hiring-manager role in the personnel recruiting application, the **opening request** and the **resumes** of candidates are the application objects most frequently interacted with. The hiring process goes through the steps of screening the applicants, interviewing candidates, and contemplating an offer with **resumes** as the primary focus of each step. We should keep resumes as the primary application objects that are linked to the secondary objects of the interview schedule, the job offer, and so on.

2 In the file-transfer application, the local files and remote files and directories are most frequently interacted with by a user. Therefore, the primary application objects should be the **files** and **directories** on the remote host and the local host.

Execution Order. Once we establish the priority based on the access frequency/duration, we also need to consider the state dependencies among application objects. We can derive the execution order of application objects from the event sequence. If the execution order is different from the access frequency priority, we need to provide appropriate contextual user interface design (e.g., visual cues, status messages, context sensitive help).

E X A M P L E   7 – 5

In a file-transfer application, the application-object priority based on access frequency may be the **files** and **directories** on the remote host and the local host, but the execution order would require the **remote host** to be connected before performing any file-transfer operation. To accommodate these different factors, we may still designate the remote files and the local files as the primary objects, but no file-transfer action can be applied before a remote host is connected.

7.3.3 Prioritizing Dynamic Relationships

Although the dynamic relationships among application objects are modeled as an element of the object model in the previous chapter, a user would still view them as user actions launched from an application object. As presented in the last section, the priority of application objects was established with information on execution order and access frequency, which are essentially scenarios of operations and dynamic relationships in typical user sessions.

The criteria for the priority of dynamic relationships are similar to that of the application objects. More frequently executed dynamic relationships and their order of execution reveal their priority in a user's application session.

E X A M P L E   7 – 6

In the file-transfer application, the execution order is:

1 *Connect to* remote host.
2 *Change to* destination directory.
3 *Transfer* files *between* hosts.
4 *Disconnect from* remote host.

The access frequency in a typical application session would have the following order:

1 *Transfer* files *between* hosts.
   User may transfer many files to or from a directory.
2 *Change to* destination directory.

User may change to different destination directories to transfer files.

3 ***Connect to*** *remote host.*
User may disconnect from current connection and reconnect to another remote host to transfer files.

7.3.4 Prioritizing Operations of Classes

Operations of a class also need to be prioritized. The execution order and the access frequency of individual operations determine their priority.

The execution order for operations of a class may depend on state transitions or data flows within the class. For example, before an object instance is created, no operation can be performed on the object. Also, until a user cuts or copies some object into the clipboard, the paste operation cannot be performed.

The access frequency of an operation varies widely with a user's task scenarios. Without statistical information from actual user usability testing or simulation of a functional GUI application, access frequency is estimated based on developers' judgment.

7.4 Logical Grouping of Object-Model Elements

Once the object elements of dynamic relationships and operations are prioritized, we need to organize further the object-model elements by grouping them into logical groups. The attributes of a class also need to be organized into logical groups. The menu-bar items in various vendor-specific GUI styles are good examples of logical groups: for example, the **File**, **Edit**, and **View** groups. We may also divide a group further into subgroups to help the user locate a menu item (Raap and Roske-Hofstrand 1988).

7.5 Error-Prevention and -Recovery Behavior

Users may make mistakes throughout their application sessions. For beginners, the frequency of errors can be so high that it amounts to a good percentage of overall task duration. There can be several levels of error-handling mechanisms in a GUI application. Here we will consider the ways to prevent the users from making mistakes. We will also discuss the error-recovery behavior of GUI applications at the system level.

7.5.1 Allow Modeless Control Actions

As a user makes a mistake, the process to recover from the error mainly involves going back to the state that existed before the erroneous execution path was started, and then reexecuting the task with the correct path. For some system-level dynamic relationships where it may be impossible to recover completely from an error, some corrective path can still be taken to remedy the impact. Let's consider an example of error scenarios.

E X A M P L E   7 – 7
_____

In the file-transfer application, a user connected to a remote host changes to destination directory, but is unable to find the files that need to be transferred.
The error scenarios and their recovery involve the following possibilities:

1 If the destination directory is the wrong place, the user changes to the correct directory.
2 If the remote host is the wrong one, the user would have to disconnect and reconnect to the correct remote host.
_____

The error scenarios reveal the needs of a user to perform recovery actions before reexecuting the correct actions. These recovery actions must be made available to the user even when no error has been made. Without being able to access the recovery actions, a user would be stuck in the error state. Modeless control actions allow user access to recovery actions, regardless of the current state of a user's application session.

7.5.2 Disable Unavailable Control Actions

As we have seen in prioritizing class relationships and operations, the dependency from state transitions and data flows may require a specific order of execution. To enforce the execution orders and to prevent users from making mistakes, operations and dynamic relationships should be unavailable to users until their respective dependencies are satisfied.

In Chapter 10, when we discuss contextual GUI design, we will cover how to disable control actions (i.e., operations and dynamic relationships) dynamically in a GUI design.

7.5.3 Provide Undo/Redo Action

Undo action allows a user to back out of a wrong path, while restoring the previous states. The GUI application is taking a more proactive role in recovering user errors with this method. The design and implementation of an undo mechanism should always be considered an important task of a GUI application development.

In object-oriented GUI, the mechanism of undo action can be implemented as an operation in individual classes, along with a global control flow that invokes the appropriate operations in the affected objects (Wang and Green 1991).

However, there are some user actions that cannot be recovered easily—for example, when an electronic mail is sent, or a file is printed. When the hiring manager realizes that a resume has been forwarded to the wrong person, it is too late to recall the forwarding action.

7.5.4   Confirm Irrecoverable Actions

In some situations, we can minimize the possibility of a user taking an irrecoverable action, such as overwriting an existing file, disconnecting from remote host, or removing all the files in a directory. Once a user performs these actions, it will be difficult to recover the losses. Users should be warned of the consequences, and a confirmation should be granted before the application can proceed with the destructive action.

7.6   CASE STUDY: A PERSONNEL RECRUITING APPLICATION

In this section, we continue studying the personnel recruiting application by conducting user interface system-level design. The system-level user interface design partitions the user interface-level object model on user-group boundaries, and then prioritizes the elements in a object model.

7.6.1   Partitioning a User Interface-Level Object Model

Specific to this application, the user analysis identified that user role is the dominating difference factor. We should partition the object model on the boundaries that separate each user role. In Figure 7-5, the classes are divided by the user roles that access them. Depending on the class and the user role, some classes are shared among more than one user role, and some classes have limited access by different user roles. Only write access will allow users to create/edit/delete an object instance. This requires that we further abstract these classes into the general read-only superclasses and the specialized writable subclasses.

Also in Figure 7-5, the lowercase letters in the square brackets denote objects' accessibility by the specific user roles (e.g., [w] for write-access), the bold capital letters indicate the user role (e.g., **H** for the hiring manager, **R** for the recruiter). Each user role has read-access to all classes listed with user roles positioned above it—for example, the hiring manager has read-access to classes listed with administrator and committee member roles.

7.6.2   Prioritizing and Grouping Object-Model Elements

Prioritizing and grouping object-model elements allow us to organize them into windows of information, which are displayed in response to user interaction. For the user role of system administrator, the **user account** is the only class to be write accessed. But for other user roles, the user accesses object instances of several application classes throughout the task performing sessions. Prioritizing and grouping the object-model elements are necessary for these user roles.

For the other hiring committee members, the execution order and access

Administrator	User account [w]		
Committee member	Cases		
	Case [**R** w] Interviewees [**H** w] Job requirements [**H** w]		
	Interviewee Resume [**R** w]		
	Interview schedule [**R** w]		
	Interview assessment [w]		
Hiring manager	Opening request [w] Candidates [w] New hire [w]		
	Committee [w] Candidate Job offer [w, **R** w]		
Recruiter	Applicants [w] Job application		
	Applicant		

Figure 7–5.   Partitioning of object model based on user role difference.

frequency/duration of classes are shown in Figure 7-6. Their involvement in the recruiting process is limited; the **resume** and the **assessment** of an interviewee are most frequently accessed objects.

Execution Order:

user account ▸ cases ▸ interviewees ⟨ interview schedule / resume / interview assessment

Frequency/Duration

resume, interview assessment

Figure 7–6.   Execution order and access frequency/duration of classes for the hiring committee member user role.

The user role of hiring manager accesses more classes than other hiring committee members. This is to allow the hiring manager to specify opening requests, make critical screening decisions, and prepare the job offer. We show the execution order and access frequency/duration of classes for the hiring manager user role in Figure 7-7. Depending on the different task scenarios, different execution order and access frequency/duration may emerge as circled items 1, 2, 3, and 4 in this figure.

The user role of personnel recruiter is the frequent user of the recruiting application. Personnel recruiters handle multiple opening requests simultaneously to serve the needs of several hiring managers at a time. Their job functions include setting up a file for each opening case, screening applicants to find

Execution order

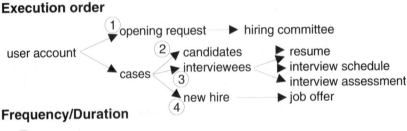

Frequency/Duration

(1) opening request, hiring committee

(2) resume, candidates

(3) resume, assessment, interviewees, interview schedule

(4) job offer, new hire

Figure 7–7.   Execution order and access frequency/duration of classes
for the hiring manager user role.

qualified candidates, scheduling interviews for interviewees with hiring committee members, and working with a hiring manager to prepare a job-offer package.
In Figure 7-8, we show the execution order and access frequency/duration for
each possible task scenario for the recruiter user role. As in Figure 7-7, the circled items indicate possible task scenarios.

Execution order

Frequency/Duration

(1) opening request, case
(2) opening request, resume, applicants
(3) interview schedule, hiring committee, interviewees
(4) job offer

Figure 7–8.   Execution order and access frequency/duration of classes
for the recruiter user role.

Once we have established the priority and logical grouping of classes for
each user role, we then focus on other object-model elements—relationships,
operations, attributes, and alternative views—for each individual class. We reor-

ganize the class diagram to reflect the priority and logical grouping, as shown in Table 7-1.

Table 7–1 Priority and Logical Grouping for the Object Model of Personnel Recruiting Application.

Object	Relationship	Operation	Attribute	Facet	Alternative View
opening request	1. has requirement 2. is sent to recruiter	1. open 2. close 3. browse 4. create 5. edit 6. delete	1. title 2. priority 3. hiring manager 4. job responsibility	1. all possible job titles in a department 2. low/ medium/ high 3. extracted from user account information 4. textual statements	1. a single view containing all attributes 2. a view using the **forms** metaphor
job applicant	1. has resume 2. applies for an opening	1. create 2. select 3. delete	1. name 2. status 3. availability	1. from resume 2. candidate/to be interviewed/ interviewed 3. date	1. name attribute only view 2. name and status view 3. name, status, and availability view
.					
.					
.					

The priority and logical grouping we established in Table 7-1 have enabled us to refine further the user interface-level object model of the personnel recruiting application to reflect this information. In the next chapter, we will conduct the user interface metaphor design to map to this refined user interface-level object model.

7.7 SUMMARY

In this chapter, we have presented user interface system-level design. By focusing on a situation where user role is the dominating difference factor, we partitioned the user interface-level object model based on user roles. We then prioritized classes, identified possible concurrent classes, and prioritized other elements of the object model by enumerating task scenarios in the task model. We also discussed other user interface system-level design consideration of user error prevention and recovery behavior. We continued studying the personnel recruiting application by partitioning the user interface-level object model, prioritizing classes and other elements of the object model.

The individual life-cycle activities in our approach are highly iterative in practice. The results of analysis activities may have to be revised periodically based on new findings in subsequent activities. As we entered the user interface system-level design activity, we have reexamined the task model by enumerating task scenarios, as well as the user interface-level object model by partitioning it on user group boundaries. We should revise the task model to include newly discovered task scenarios, while the user interface-level object model should reflect the priorities and logical groups of classes and other elements of the object model.

In the next chapter, we will cover user interface metaphor design activity, which will benefit from the fact that we have partitioned the user interface-level object model and prioritized classes and other object-model elements. In Chapter 9, as we present object-oriented GUI design, the priority and logical grouping of object-model elements will determine the display sequence of windows, and the organization of object information in windows.

C H A P T E R **8**

User Interface Metaphor Design

*T*he linguistic term *metaphor* has become a popular term in the practice of user interface designs. Cognitive psychology and artificial intelligence studies use the similar term *analogy* to explain the human learning and problem-solving processes. The value of user interface metaphors lies in the analogy it provides for the users that helps them to learn the application and to perform tasks.

In this chapter, we address the important features of user interface metaphors: experiential, structured, selective, extensible, and coherent (or consistent). We then present a user interface metaphor design procedure that starts with identifying possible metaphors, then mapping candidate metaphors to the target application, and finally evaluating the mapping to select a source metaphor. To provide a notation for a metaphor-mapped user interface-level object model, we simply rename object-model elements with source-metaphor domain terminology. Continuing the case study of a personnel recruiting application, we take the user interface-level object model refined in the user interface system-level design and select a source metaphor for it.

8.1 WHY USER INTERFACE METAPHORS?

A number of mental models have been proposed to explain the human learning and problem-solving process (Carroll and Olson 1988). In recent years, the important role of analogy in human learning, reasoning, and problem-solving processes has become widely recognized (Anderson 1989, 1990).

The phenomena of analogical reasoning and problem solving explain how humans learn and solve problems from examples and familiar experiences (Holyoak and Thagard 1989; Clement and Gentner 1991). Lately, a number of computational models of analogical reasoning have been proposed in artificial intelligence studies in an attempt to emulate the human learning and problem-solving process (Hall 1989). Although the discussion of computational models is well beyond the scope of this book, the results of these studies strongly reconfirm the important role of the user interface metaphor in helping users to learn and to solve problems with a new application.

By presenting applications with an underlying user interface metaphor, beginning users will have a much easier time learning a new application. Occasional users will also be able to rely on the user interface metaphor to recall various ways of using an application. As their skill levels grow with more practice, experienced- and expert-level users may also try to go beyond their current comprehension of a user interface metaphor structure to find better ways of working with an application.

User interface developers need to understand the essentials of user interface metaphors, their accompanying limitations, and the metaphor design procedure.

8.2 CRITERIA OF USER INTERFACE METAPHORS

Metaphors have a number of inherent characteristics. Studies in linguistics have found that the linguistic metaphors reveal many of the human thought processes, similar to the findings in cognitive science and artificial intelligence (Lakoff and Johnson 1980; Lakoff 1987; Johnson 1987). Metaphors are experiential, structured, selective, extensible, and coherent. In the following sections, we consider these characteristics and their implications in the user interface metaphor design.

8.2.1 Experiential

A user won't be able to comprehend the meaning of metaphors in a user interface application if he or she does not have the relevant prior experience of the specific source metaphor domain. We should consider the sociocultural and application-domain skill-level differences among users in order to devise candidate metaphors that are experiential.

EXAMPLE   8 − 1

---

1 The *ftp* (file transfer program) on UNIX systems has the commands to connect a
remote host, change directories, transfer files, and set file-transfer mode. The users
must be skilled programmers who understand the computer networking, and the
UNIX file system. A user without this prior knowledge will have a hard time learning this application.

2 If we were to devise a *file repository* metaphor for the same program, the users who
are familiar with the file-repository operation will be able to learn the application
easily. On the other hand, those who don't know anything about a file repository will
have a hard time learning the application.

Design Guidelines

- **Emulate application-domain systems.** Use the existing application-
domain system, if there is one, as the metaphor. A library-material search
application may use the library index-card metaphor. An accounting application may use the metaphors of journals, ledgers, and forms of invoices. The
example of the personnel recruiting application computerizes the recruiting
process with the forms of opening request and applicants' resumes.

- **Match users' sociocultural experiences.** Depending on the nature of an
application, it may be difficult to come up with a metaphor that can generally be comprehended by users with different sociocultural backgrounds.
We may have to devise different metaphors for each target user group.

8.2.2   Structured

To select a metaphor (or metaphors), we examine the mapping of each candidate source metaphor onto the target application to find the best match. The
metaphor-mapping process establishes structural correspondence between the
source metaphor and the target application (Falkenhainer et al 1989). For an
application's object-model representation, this structure consists of the application objects and the relationships among them. Figure 8-1 depicts the structural
correspondence of metaphor mapping.

EXAMPLE   8 − 2

---

1 The *file-cabinet* metaphor has been widely used to represent the tree-structured
computer file systems. The hierarchies of file cabinets, drawers, holders, folders,
and files are mapped onto computer file system's root directory, subdirectories, and
files. Although the objects don't have exact mapping from the source metaphor to
the target application (a computer file system directory may contain files as well as
directories), the structural relationship of file hierarchy and categorization make
the metaphor a popular choice among user interface designers.

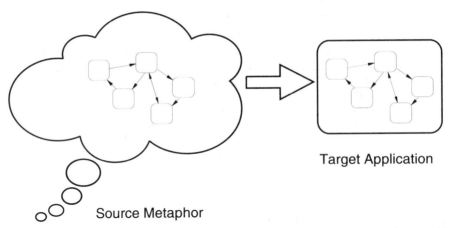

Target Application

Source Metaphor

Figure 8–1. A structured source metaphor has structural correspondence with the target application object model.

2 The *workbench* metaphor has been used for software applications that provide development tools in an integrated software environment. The hammers, chisels, and pliers certainly don't map clearly onto the compiler, debugger, and profiler components. However, the notion of a workbench with the necessary tools offers a good structural mapping to an integrated software development environment with its software development tools.

Design Guidelines

- **Map objects to convey structural relationships.**
  Although the structural relationships are the primary concern in the metaphor-mapping process, they may not be represented explicitly in user interface designs, but are rather implicitly conveyed through the presentation of objects. The application objects must find their corresponding metaphor objects that maintain the structural relationships.
- **Map structural relationships among metaphor objects.**
  We then focus on the mapping of structural relationships among metaphor objects, not the individual attributes of objects. Primary structural relationships among target application objects must find their corresponding mapping in the source metaphor.

8.2.3   Partial and Selective

Depending on its relevance to a target application, only part of a metaphor's structure has to be mapped selectively. The metaphor-mapping process also emphasizes the structural relationships and objects, not the object attributes and operations. In Figure 8-2, the source metaphor domain is the larger light-shaded area, and the smaller unshaded area inside represents the part being mapped to the target application. The margin between the perimeter of a target application and the mapped metaphor is to denote the partial and selective nature of metaphor mapping.

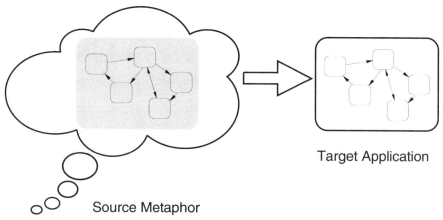

Target Application

Source Metaphor

Figure 8–2. Only part of a metaphor is selectively mapped to the target application.

EXAMPLE   8 – 3

We can find a number of low-cost graphic design applications on personal computer platforms. The *painting* metaphor is a popular choice for these applications. A target application adopting this metaphor typically features a number of painting tools (such as airbrush, paint brush, paint roller, and pencil) along with a color palette and a drawing canvas. As a low-end application, it doesn't differentiate between watercolor and oil painting, the variety of the drawing canvas material, or other choices of painting tools. Figure 8-3 shows such an example.

Design Guidelines

- **Candidate source metaphors are partially and selectively mapped to the target application.**
  Candidate source metaphors can represent concepts that are well beyond the scope of the target application. During the metaphor mapping process, we selectively map only part of the source metaphor that would correspond to the target-application object model.

8.2.4   Extensible

As users learn a new application and are mentally undergoing the metaphor-mapping process, they may extend the metaphor to try new ways of using

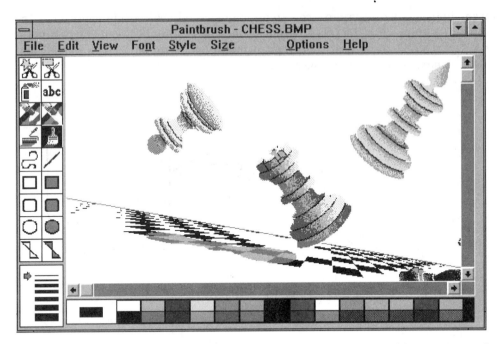

Figure 8–3. A graphic drawing program uses the painting metaphor. The painting tools are on the left. The color palette is at the bottom.

the application. A user's metaphor-extension process involves establishing new structural relationships among existing (or new) application objects. In artificial intelligence studies, the metaphor-extension process is considered as inferencing from existing predicates (Hall 1989).

In Figure 8-4, the objects and structural relationships are represented as round-corner boxes and lines (heavy lines for mapped metaphor, and dotted lines for extended metaphor). The extended metaphorical relationships and objects may fall outside the target application-domain mapping, because target applications only provide well-defined functions. The extensions falling inside the target application-domain indicate a possible oversight during object-modeling activity.

Design Guidelines

- **Consider metaphor extensions to discover new relationships.**
  Although a metaphor is partially and selectively mapped to a target application, considering metaphor extensions may help us in discovering additional relationships among target application objects.
- **Consider metaphor extensions to discover new objects.**
  Just as new relationships can be uncovered when we consider metaphor extensions, new target application objects may also surface. Supporting these new relationships and objects in the target application may be crucial to validate the coherence of composite metaphors (introduced in the next section).

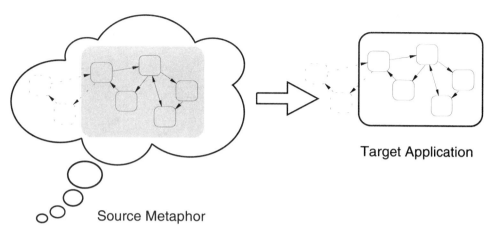

Figure 8–4. Metaphors are extensible. Extensions may fall inside or outside the target application object model.

8.2.5 Consistent or Coherent

For a large and complex target application, the different aspects of the application can be viewed as some substructures of its object model. If a single metaphor can be identified that maps well into all aspects of a target application, the subparts of this metaphor are *consistent*. However, it can be difficult to find a single metaphor that maps well onto a large application. One may have to identify multiple metaphors to map onto the different aspects of a complex target application. The multiple metaphors forming the composite metaphor of an application must be related with each other in order to qualify as *coherent* metaphors. Composite metaphors are interconnected with direct structural relationships. These intermetaphor relationships ensure the coherence of composite metaphors, which is essential for user comprehension of a complex application. We can view coherent metaphors as substructures of a conceptually broader metaphor.

In Figure 8-5, metaphors A and B are part of metaphor C, and therefore are consistent metaphors; while in Figure 8-6, metaphor A and metaphor B are distinct but interconnected with structural relationship extension (the dotted line between the two metaphors), and therefore are coherent metaphors.

E X A M P L E   8 – 4

---

1 A *calendar* metaphor and a *notepad* metaphor are both part of the *desktop* metaphor, and therefore are consistent metaphors.
2 A *mail* metaphor is coherent with the *desktop* metaphor, because of its direct connection with desktop metaphor subparts of *in-basket* and *out-basket* metaphors.

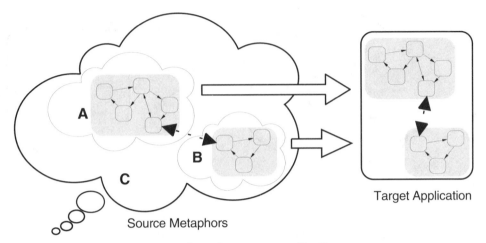

Figure 8–5. Consistent metaphors for a target application.

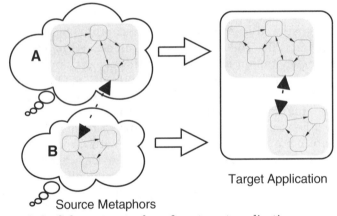

Figure 8–6. Coherent metaphors for a target application.

Design Guidelines

- **Composite metaphors are subsets of a broader metaphor.**
  Structured metaphors must be substructures of a larger structured metaphor to allow for establishing consistency among composite metaphors.

- **Composite metaphors are directly connected.**
  As substructures of a larger structured metaphor, composite metaphors are interconnected either directly, or indirectly through structural extensions. To make sure that the composite metaphors are apparent to the users, the interconnections should be directly connected, and the users shouldn't have to mentally extend the metaphors to find connections.

8.3 LIMITATIONS OF USER INTERFACE METAPHORS

With appropriate metaphor design, users can quickly learn to use a new application effectively by using their own prior knowledge and experience. But when there are diverse user groups, we may have to design user interfaces with multiple metaphors, which would require additional development resources. Metaphor mismatches in user interface design may also cause negative experiences for users.

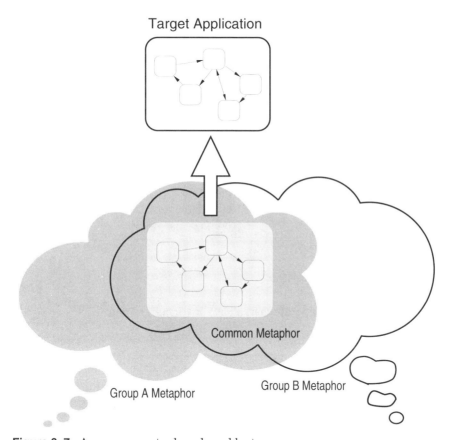

Figure 8–7. A common metaphor shared by two user groups.

8.3.1 Diverse User Groups

Since metaphors are highly experiential, an application targeting diverse user groups should present a common metaphor that is shareable among these groups, as shown in Figure 8-7. However, depending on the application, it is possible the user groups don't have any relevant shared experience among them. If this is the case, we then have to use separate metaphors to address the specific user groups (see Figure 8-8). Both approaches require careful thought and extensive user feedback. Although the common-metaphor approach requires much less development effort, it may be difficult to devise. On the other hand, it is easier to identify separate metaphors for individual groups, but the development and maintenance effort may become prohibitively large.

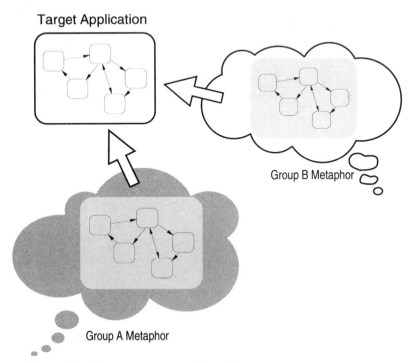

Target Application

Group B Metaphor

Group A Metaphor

Figure 8–8. Two separate metaphors for two users groups.

E X A M P L E   8 – 5

The *ftp* example discussed in Section 8.2.1 has a number of candidate metaphors. For the user group of programmers, the present system works just fine. The operations of connecting a remote host, changing directories, transferring files, and setting the file-transfer mode are all very familiar to programmers. On the other hand, for other groups of users, a *file-repository* metaphor is much more familiar.

Since a newly devised metaphor (i.e., the *file-repository* metaphor) is not likely to map as closely as the predecessor-system-based metaphor, the *file-repository* metaphor can become a hindrance for the programmer user group in performing its task. If both groups are targeted as the primary markets, the GUI application will have to support two separate metaphors.

8.3.2   Metaphor Mismatches and Shortfalls

Metaphor mismatch occurs when parts of the source metaphor structure do not have the corresponding target-application counterparts. Metaphor shortfall defines a situation where the source metaphor cannot encompass the entire target-application structure.

The computer software technology allows a target application to support a number of features that do not resemble any real-world experience of many user groups. Even the user interface metaphor design activity has identified the best-matched metaphor(s). Mismatches and shortfalls are still common between the selected source metaphor and the target application.

Metaphor mismatches and shortfalls cause user misconceptions about the target-application functions, and this will lead to many user errors and underutilized features. Although these situations can be somewhat remedied by providing on line context-sensitive error and help messages, they are the sore spots of a user interface application.

E X A M P L E   8 – 6

1 When the *file-cabinet* metaphor is mapped onto the UNIX file system, the mismatches and shortfalls shown in Table 8-1 occur.

2 The object-oriented drawing applications provide some very powerful features that allow users to perform complex manipulation of drawing objects. The operations of resizing, stretching, rotating, and enveloping, along with many others, far exceed any source metaphor from the traditional drawing tools, even though a well-trained draftsperson regularly performs these operations mentally. The direct manipulation, object-oriented source metaphor of these applications provides users with a whole new experience, which will in turn become the familiar source metaphor of many other new target applications.

Table 8–1 Mismatches and Shortfalls Between Source Metaphor and Target Application

Source Metaphor	Target Application
Monolithic hierarchies of file cabinet, file drawer, file holder, and file folder.	Each level of the tree-structured directory hierarchy contains both flat files and subdirectories.
Each cabinet has a lock for security.	The file system has access control at both the directory and file level.
No correspondence.	Files and directories can be symbolically linked to other parts of the file system.

8.4 USER INTERFACE METAPHOR DESIGN PROCEDURE

In the previous sections, we have discussed the design guidelines to follow, and pitfalls to avoid in user interface metaphor design activity. Throughout, we have described the structured source metaphor as a network of objects that are interconnected with structural relationships.

As discussed in the previous section, user interface metaphors must be experiential, structured, selective, extensible, and coherent. The candidate metaphors must satisfy the criteria of a user interface metaphor to qualify as a usable metaphor. We discussed a number of design guidelines in the second section of this chapter. The design procedure reflects these metaphor design guidelines.

To formalize the user interface metaphor design procedure to enable it to fit in with other activities of our approach, we will use the object model of the target application to represent the metaphor-mapping process. We can reflect the priority of a target application's objects and relationships by assigning weighting factors to them. We will select the source metaphor with the highest score in the mapping process.

In the following sections, we will examine how to identify the candidate source metaphors; the object model representation of the metaphor-mapping process; a simple scoring for the metaphor evaluation process; and the extensions and mismatches of a selected source metaphor.

8.4.1   Identifying Candidate Metaphors or Composite Metaphors

The first step of user interface metaphor design is to identify a number of candidate metaphors. There are several possible sources.

Application-Domain Metaphors. The best candidate metaphors come from the application domain and are highly experiential for experienced- and expert-level application-domain-skilled users. For any application domain, users are trained to be experienced or expert in application-domain skill to perform their job functions effectively.

Emulating Present System.   Closely emulate the present system that is going to be replaced by the target application, especially if the target market consists largely of users of the present system.

Existing Graphical Environment Metaphors.   For applications that are developed as a new component in an integrated application environment, candidate metaphors can be derived from extending existing environment metaphors. For example, an office-automation target application can use candidate source metaphors that are coherent or consistent (see Section 8.2.5) with the existing *desktop* metaphor in the target windowing environment.

Prior Experiences.   For applications that are highly innovative, there may not be any existing application-domain knowledge, present system, or user windowing environment metaphors to draw from. Through user interviews, testing, and feedback, highly experiential metaphors can be derived from their experiences.

8.4.2   Mapping Candidate Metaphors onto the Object Model

The metaphor-mapping process focuses on the structural relationships among application objects. An object model contains the information of target-application objects and structural relationships, along with other details irrelevant to the metaphor-mapping process.

To accomplish the one-to-one mapping process, we follow the steps below:

1   List target-application objects based on their system-level behavioral priority.
2   Find the corresponding source-metaphor object for each application object.
3   List the prioritized target-application relationships.
4   Find the corresponding source-metaphor relationships for each of the target-application relationships.

E X A M P L E   8 – 7

We have two candidate source metaphors for the *ftp* application—a *file repository* metaphor and a library metaphor. Table 8-2 has three columns—one for the target application and the other two for the source metaphors. Also, the top rows map objects, and the bottom rows map structural relationships.

Table **8–2** Mapping Source Metaphors to the Target Application

Target Application	*File-Repository* Metaphor	*Library* Metaphor
files	files	books, materials
tree structured file paths	file cabinets, file drawers	bookshelves
remote hosts	repository sites	libraries
user account password	access badge	library card
get files from a remote host	get copies of files from a repository	check out copies of materials from a library
put files to a remote host	put files to a repository	check in copies of materials to a library
change file path	move to another drawer	move to another shelf
connect to a remote host	go to a repository site	go to a library

8.4.3   Evaluating Candidate Metaphors

Once the one-to-one correspondence of objects and relationships between the target application and source metaphors are found, we need to evaluate the mappings to select the best metaphor. Depending on the priority of the objects and relationships, we can assign a weighting factor to each of them and give a score based on the quality of each match. The metaphor with the highest total score is the best choice.

E X A M P L E   8 - 8

For the same *ftp* application, we assign a weighting factor and a score to each item, as shown in Table 8-3. The weighting factors are based on the priority of the individual item, and the scores are based on the quality of mapping correspondence. We will select the metaphor with the highest total score as the source metaphor for the target application. The tree-structured file system does not have good correspondence in the source metaphors. Also, the dynamic relationships of get/put files from a remote host do not match well with the *library* metaphor. The final score shows the *file-repository* metaphor to be the better choice.

Table 8–3 Assigning Weighting Factors and Scores

Target Application	*File Repository* Metaphor		*Library* Metaphor	
files	10/10	files	10/10	books, materials
tree-structured file paths	7/10	file cabinets, file drawers	4/10	bookshelves
remote hosts	5/5	repository sites	5/5	libraries
user account	3/3	access badge	2/3	library card
get files from a remote host	10/10	get copies of files from a repository	7/10	check out copies of materials from a library
put files to a remote host	10/10	put files to a repository	7/10	check in copies of materials to a library
change file path	7/10	move to another drawer	5/10	move to another shelf
connect to a remote host	8/8	go to a repository site	8/8	go to a library

8.4.4   Considering Metaphor Extensions and Mismatches

As users establish their mental models of an application based on the metaphor, they may extend the metaphor and go on expecting many application functions that are most likely not supported. Because of this type of false expectations, metaphor mismatches can cause constant user errors and frustration.

After a metaphor is selected, we must consider the implications of metaphor extensions and mismatches in order to compensate for any side effects on the user interface design.

E X A M P L E   8 − 9

As we have selected the *file-repository* metaphor for the ftp application, a number of metaphor extensions come to mind. With a large amount of files in storage, file repositories must support some indexing system to ease the file-searching task. However, the ftp application does not support the searching function, which is really a very useful feature to have.

8.5 NOTATION FOR METAPHOR-MAPPED OBJECT MODEL

We have discussed user interface metaphor design procedure that maps candidate source metaphors onto the user interface-level object model. In order to document the metaphor-mapped user interface-level object model, you can continue using your favorite object-model notation by simply replacing the names of each object-model element with source-metaphor terminology in a replicated copy of a user interface-level object model. In the situation of multiple metaphors or design iterations, the original version of the object model can be remapped.

8.6 GUI REPRESENTATION OF METAPHORS

With all the effort spent on selecting a source metaphor, the user interface metaphor design is not complete until the source metaphor is properly conveyed through GUI representation.

As we have discussed earlier, the objects and the structural relationships among them are the key factors in evaluating the source-to-target mapping. We also realize that the application objects are the explicit focus of attention throughout a user's application session. Therefore, the GUI representation of the objects and their relationships must reflect the underlying source metaphor.

A user interface-level object model also includes the elements of operations and attributes. Although, in order to keep the mapping process simple, we have not considered these elements in selecting a source metaphor, their consistent representation with metaphor-mapped objects and structural relationships would reinforce the notion of a source metaphor.

In the next chapter, we will discuss the object-oriented GUI design of an application. We will also cover the comprehensive representation of a metaphor-mapped user interface-level object model.

8.7 CASE STUDY: A PERSONNEL RECRUITING APPLICATION

We have refined the user interface-level object model for this application in the last chapter to reflect the priority and logical grouping of object-model elements. In this section, we move on to the next step to conduct user interface metaphor design activity. In the next subsections, we follow the design procedure covered in this chapter to identify candidate metaphors and evaluate the object-model mapping to make metaphor design decisions.

We conduct metaphor design for each user role involved. We also reference the user analysis result to design metaphors according to the characteristics of the specific user role.

8.7.1 Identifying Candidate Metaphors

Depending on the user role, users have different perceptions of the personnel recruiting process. The system administrators have expert-level computer skills. Since they maintain user accounts for this application and interact only with the **user-account** objects, a good candidate metaphor for the system administrator role is a *computer system account-administration* metaphor.

The user roles of hiring committee member, hiring manager, and recruiter require application-domain-specific metaphors to help them perform their tasks.

1 **Application-domain metaphors**

   Although the application-domain metaphor is necessary for the hiring committee member, hiring manager, and recruiter user roles, it is comprehended differently depending on the user role. As the results of user analysis have shown, users with the recruiter role have experienced- or expert-level application-domain knowledge, while the hiring manager has much less application-domain knowledge, and other hiring committee members have only limited knowledge of recruiting process.

   We use partial application-domain metaphors as candidate metaphors for the hiring manager and other hiring committee members. A complete recruiting-process domain metaphor will be the candidate metaphor for the recruiter role. As shown in Figure 8-9, the candidate metaphor for the hiring-committee member role is the *interview-process* metaphor, which is partial to the larger-scope *screening-process* metaphor for the hiring-manager role, which in turn is partial to the *recruiting-process* metaphor for the recruiter role. Looking at it from another perspective, the *recruiting-process* metaphor is a composite metaphor that includes the *screening-process* metaphor. Similarly, the *screening-process* metaphor is a composite metaphor that includes the *interview-process* metaphor.

2 **Emulate existing systems**

   Without an automated software application, the recruiting process goes on with different kinds of paper *forms*, scribbled *notes*, paper copies of *resumes*, interview *schedule sheets*, and verbal communication. These are all good candidate metaphors, which are also partial metaphors of the *recruiting-process* metaphor derived from the application domain.

3 **Existing graphical environment metaphors**

   The application is also operated under a larger GUI environment that coexists with other software tools such as *electronic mail* and *calendar* pro-

Figure 8–9. Candidate metaphors from the application domain.

grams. We can consider the *electronic mail* and *calendar* as candidate
metaphors by simply integrating the application with these existing programs. Even if these candidate metaphors are not selected after the evaluation process, the final selected metaphors should be coherent with the
existing metaphors in the graphical environment if possible.

8.7.2 Mapping Candidate Metaphors onto the Object Model

Because the user interface-level object model was constructed from the user
task model, much of the candidate metaphor derived from the application
domain is already captured in the object model without further metaphor mapping. In Figure 8-10, we use the object model to show the metaphor mapping.
Metaphors are denoted with italics enclosd in parentheses (e.g., *interview process, forms*). Note that the *forms* metaphor is used for the job-opening request
and interview assessment. The same as in Figure 7-5, the lowercase letters in
the square brackets denote objects' accessibility by the specific user roles (e.g.,
[w] for write-accessible); the bold capital letters indicate the user role (e.g., **H** for
the hiring manager, **R** for the recruiter).

8.7.3 Evaluating Candidate Metaphors

Since we have considered metaphors derived from the application domain
and existing system (the best sources of candidate metaphors for such an application), the metaphor mapping to the target-application object model showed
close matches in many respects. There is no need to go through a scoring process
to compare different candidate metaphors in this case. We simply adopt this metaphor and map it to the refined user interface-level object model.

It is also significant that, since the user interface-level object model was

Administrator *(computer account administration)*	User account [w]		

Committee member
(interview process)
	Cases
	  Case [**R** w] Interviewees [**H** w] Job requirements [**H** w]
	           Interviewee Resume [**R** w]
	           Interview schedule [**R** w] *(calendar, schedule sheet)*
	           Interview assessment [w] *(forms)*		

Hiring manager *(screening process)*	Opening request [w] *(forms)* Candidates [w] New hire [w] Committee [w] Candidate Job offer [w, **R** w]		
Recruiter *(recruiting process)*	Applicants [w] Job application Applicant		

Figure 8–10. Mapping metaphors to the objects in an object model.

constructed from the user task model, much of the application-domain metaphor is already captured in the object model without further metaphor mapping, as we have shown in the previous section.

Since the interview process metaphor is part of the screening process metaphor, which in turn is part of the recruiting process metaphor, these metaphors are *consistent* as we have defined in Section 2.5 of this chapter.

8.7.4   Considering Metaphor Extensions and Mismatches

For the personnel department, the recruiting application can be integrated with more extensive automated personnel operations that may include employee appraisal and compensation management. Since personnel department staff will be the primary users of such a highly integrated application system, metaphor extension should be considered for the selected recruiter role's metaphor. The *recruiting-process* metaphor for the recruiter role is derived from the application domain itself and is a partial metaphor of a *personnel-operations* metaphor. This metaphor is highly extensible to include other operations in the application domain.

Because the original purpose of this personnel recruiting application was to automate the recruiting process, we have selected candidate metaphors derived from the application domain and the existing system. The only mismatches result from the nature of computer automation such as the user-account objects, which are crucial for maintaining proper confidentiality for the recruiting process, but lack a counterpart in the source-metaphor domain. The user also cannot write *scribbled notes* of their assessment on the displayed resumes as they do on paper copies of resumes, so we have provided an *interview-assessment-form* metaphor instead.

8.8 SUMMARY

In this chapter, we discussed the user interface metaphor design activity. We explained the value of user interface metaphor in helping users learn an application. We then presented the essential features of the user interface metaphor—experiential, structured, selective, extensible, and coherent. We covered the limitations of user interface metaphors, which often arise in practice because of various constraints.

We discussed the design procedure of a user interface metaphor, in which we first identify candidate metaphors from a number of sources and then map the candidate metaphors to the user interface-level object model. The last step of this procedure is to evaluate the mapped metaphors to find the best match. The metaphor evaluation is based on a simple scoring scheme, with weighting factors derived from the priority of objects and structural relationships (covered in Chapter 7 on user interface system-level design).

In the case study, we continued with the personnel recruiting application. We considered the characteristics of distinct user groups and designed user interface metaphors according to the findings in user analysis (Chapter 4). We mapped a user interface metaphor to the user interface-level object model which we introduced in Chapter 6 and later refined in Chapter 7.

In the next chapter, we will continue the presentation of GUI design activities by mapping the metaphor-mapped user interface object model into style-specific GUI designs. With the high-level abstraction of a metaphor-mapped user interface-level object model, style-specific GUI design is a simple process of selecting appropriate GUI components.

8.9 BIBLIOGRAPHIC NOTES

Analogy is a key mechanism in John R. Anderson's recent theory on human learning process (Anderson 1989). The theory has evolved over the years from his many earlier studies, which found that both analogy-based induction and example-based learning rely on analogical mechanism.

Books authored by George Lakoff and Mark Johnson discussed metaphor from the linguistic and philosophical perspective (Lakoff and Johnson 1980; Johnson 1987). The 1980 publication is well written and easy to follow, with many examples explaining various features of metaphors. We have followed the terminology used in this book throughout this chapter.

Our approach to the metaphor-mapping process from source metaphor to the target application's user interface-level object model is much more practical than those used in research studies of analogical reasoning and problem solving

(Falkenhainer, Forbus, and Gentner 1989; Holyoak and Thagard 1989; Clement and Gentner 1991). We simply apply a basic theory on analogical mapping process (Gentner 1983), namely the structured mapping of objects and structural relationships. In (Carroll, Mack, and Kellog 1988), the metaphor mapping process has used the task model rather than the object model of a target application.

In artificial intelligence research, the definition of metaphorical mapping goes beyond the mapping of objects and relationships to include object attributes. Strictly speaking, the mapping process we have presented would be considered *analogical* to some researchers. However, our primary objective is to present a practical approach for practitioners developing GUI applications.

CHAPTER 9

Object-Oriented Graphical User Interface Design

In the previous chapter, we discussed the mapping of a user interface metaphor to the user interface-level object model. In this chapter, we continue the GUI design activity to map the metaphor-mapped user interface-level object model into style-specific GUI design.

A metaphor-mapped user interface-level object model is a high-level abstraction that has absorbed and reflected a lot of information found in user-analysis, task-analysis, and object-oriented-analysis activities. Regardless of any further generalization or specialization that may be necessary, this high-level abstraction remains the general representation of the GUI application.

Although there are a number of seemingly disparate vendor-specific user interface style guides, their differences are limited to the *look* and *feel* and the naming of individual user interface interaction components. The user interface interaction components specified by these style guides offer mostly similar functions. The object-action interaction model is also universally adopted among these style guides.

To map a metaphor-mapped user interface-level object model into a style-specific GUI design, we simply select appropriate GUI interaction components to represent various elements of an object model—namely, the classes, relationships, alternative views, object attributes, operations, and attribute facets.

9.1 GUI DESIGN MAPPING OF THE OBJECT MODEL

As the users use an application to perform their tasks, they interact with the GUI representation of the application objects. The relationships among objects, the operations, the attributes, and the facets of attributes are also presented to the users throughout various task-performing scenarios.

The object model of an application contains a large amount of information. To improve the human performance and to optimize display-screen utilization, object-model information needs to be presented in an orderly fashion based on priority and task context. We elaborate on these user interface design considerations as follows:

- **Human cognitive capacity**

  In Chapter 5, the task-analysis activity is based on a cognitive psychology approach. It takes human processing time to scan through the display screen to identify the object of interest, and then to find the relevant operations to perform a task. Small chunks of relevant information help users to identify an object quickly, apply an action, and accomplish a task.

- **Display-screen dimension**

  Computer graphic displays have limited pixel resolution and physical dimension. Object-model information needs to be arranged in an orderly fashion in a limited display space with easily discernible details.

- **Aesthetic attractiveness**

  Presenting the object-model information with graphical and textual information requires careful selection of fonts, colors, and layout in a GUI design (Marcus 1992). Visually well-organized graphic design helps users' comprehension of an application. Common graphic design guidelines are derived from well-known human visual-perception principles (Anderson 1990, Ch. 3). With the help of a professional graphic designer, a GUI application can be more than a productivity tool; it can be turned into an inviting application to work with.

User interface design principles described in various style guides (Apple Computer 1987, 1991; IBM 1991a; Open Software Foundation 1990a; Sun Microsystems 1990) present a number of design samples to demonstrate the orderly presentation of user interface information addressing these design considerations. These style guides follow the more general user interface design principles (Norman 1988; Laurel 1990; Thimbleby 1990; Shneiderman 1992). In the following sections, we unfold a user interface style-independent procedure for the GUI design mapping of a metaphor-mapped object model into different vendor-specific user interface styles.

9.2   GUI DESIGN MAPPING OF USER INTERFACE METAPHOR

A user interface metaphor is selected because of its close correspondence with the target application in terms of the objects and structural relationships among them. Depending on the GUI environment of a target application and the characteristics of the relationship itself, a relationship can be represented in different ways (we will examine these in Section 9.6). Generally speaking, a relationship can be implicitly reflected from the representation of the objects it is linked with, or it can be explicitly represented as an action associated with an object.

Regardless of how the relationships of an object model are represented, the objects are always the primary focus of user interactions. A user interface metaphor would be much easier for users to comprehend if it is represented in the target-application objects. In Section 9.5, we will consider the presentation of application objects and how we can convey the structural relationships that made the metaphor meaningful in the first place.

We can further reinforce the metaphor representation by properly presenting the operations, the attributes, and the facets of an object to reflect the metaphor. In Section 9.7, we consider the GUI presentation of the operations, the attributes, and the facets.

9.3   USER INTERACTION MODELS

A GUI style guide specifies interaction models with which users can interact with GUI applications. The two most common models are the object-action interaction model and the drag-and-drop interaction model.

9.3.1   Object-Action Interaction

Although a number of seemingly disparate user interface style guides have been specified by different vendors, a major commonality among them is the object-action interaction model. With the object-action interaction model, a user first selects an object(s), and then select an action to apply to the object(s). The available actions can be applied to the selected object(s) in sequence.

The object-action interaction model has been generally adopted by different style guides because this model recognizes the central role of objects in a GUI application. As the users interact with an application to perform their application tasks, they are focused on the application objects in their interaction with the application. A series of actions are selectively applied to the selected object(s) by the user to accomplish the task goals.

The actions of an object include changing the values of the attributes, applying the dynamic relationships, and performing some inherent operations. In Figure 9-1, a helicopter object is the selected object, and the pull-down menu items under the **Draw** title are some of the actions that the user can select to apply to the helicopter object. **Ungroup** is the action item being selected.

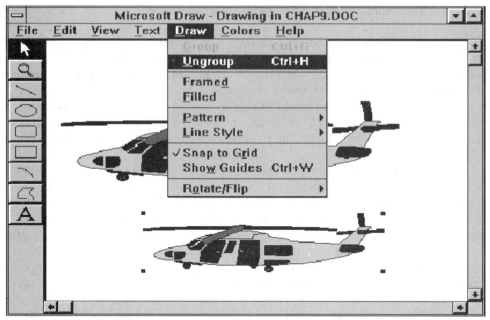

Figure 9–1. A helicopter object is bracketed with four small dark handles signifying it as being selected. The pull-down menu items are some of the actions that can be selected to apply to the selected object.

9.3.2   Drag-and-Drop Interaction

A number of user interface style guides specify the drag-and-drop interaction model to allow direct manipulation of graphical objects by user. A drag-and-drop interaction may imply a *move to*, a *copy to*, or a *link to* action, depending on the relationships between the source object (where the dragging starts) and the target object (where the dragging ends—i.e., dropping).

Although the underlying mechanism of the drag-and-drop interaction is flexible enough to allow many dynamic relationships to be effected that are beyond the simple notion of *move to*, *copy to*, or *link to*, overusing it can easily confuse the users.

9.4   STYLE-SPECIFIC GUI INTERACTION COMPONENTS

A typical user interface style guide provides user interface designers with the information on the graphical environment, the user interface design principles, and the style-specific GUI interaction components. The object-action interaction model examined in the last section is a key component of the graphical environment. The style-specific user interface interaction components offer a set of consistent graphical components for building GUI applications. Each GUI interaction component has a specific look-and-feel (i.e., appearance and behavior), and recommended usage.

With the objective of mapping an application's object model to a GUI design, a user interface designer's task is to find the logical interaction components to represent the entire object model, while conforming to a specific style guide. Even when the application portability among various graphical environments is a major design requirement, the object-model mapping remains the essential consideration.

Looking beyond the superficial differences in nomenclature, appearance, or behavior, many of the user interface components specified in different style guides are functionally equivalent. After all, the various style guides were developed with the same underlying user interface design principles in mind. To serve the same usage purposes, similar user interface interaction components are devised, although there are many original contributions in each of these style guides.

Table 9-1 lists the GUI interaction components from the Apple desktop interface (Apple Computer 1987, 1991), the Systems Application Architecture/ Common User Access (SAA/CUA) (IBM 1989, 1991a, 1991b), the NextStep Environment (NeXT, Inc. 1991), the OSF/Motif (Open Software Foundation 1991a), and the OPEN LOOK (Sun Microsystems 1990) style guides. Each row shows a functionally equivalent user interface interaction component from each style guide. A cell is left empty if there is no equivalent interaction component specified.

Table 9–1 Equivalent GUI Interaction Components among the Vendor-Specific Style Guides

	Apple	SAA/CUA	NextStep	Motif	OPEN LOOK
1.	multiple windows, split window panes and panels	multiple-document interface, workplace, split windows	main window, standard windows	multiple primary windows, multiple window panes	multiple base windows, split panes, multiple panes
2.	dialog boxes	dialog boxes	panels	dialog boxes	pop-up windows
3.	menu bar, titles, pull-down menus, menu items	menu bar, menu bar choices, pull-down menu, menu items	main menu, submenus	menu bar, titles, pull-down menus, menu selections	control area, menu buttons, button menus, menu items
4.	scrolling menus				
5.	hierarchical menus	cascaded menus	submenus	cascading menus	submenus
6.	pop-up menus	drop-down (scrolling) lists	pop-up list	option menus	abbreviated menu buttons
7.		pop-up menus		pop-up menus	pop-up menus

Table 9–1 Cont. Equivalent GUI Interaction Components among the Vendor-Specific Style Guides

Apple	SAA/CUA	NextStep	Motif	OPEN LOOK
8. tear-off menus		tear-off sub-menus	tear-off menus	menus with pushpins
9. palettes	value sets			exclusive settings
10. buttons	push buttons	push buttons	push buttons	buttons
11. check boxes	check boxes	switches (toggles)	check buttons	check boxes, non-exclusive settings
12. radio buttons	radio buttons	radio buttons	radio buttons	exclusive settings
13.	spin buttons		stepper buttons	numeric fields
14. dials (progress indicators)	progress indicators	sliders	scales	sliders, gauges
15. scroll bars	scroll bars	scrollers	scroll bars	scroll bars
16. 1-D arrays	list boxes		list boxes	scrolling lists
17.				hierarchical scrolling lists
18.	combination boxes			
19. type-in pop-up menus	drop-down combination boxes			text field with abbreviated menu buttons
20. 2-D arrays		matrix		tables
21. text fields	entry fields	text fields	text entry boxes	text fields
22.		forms		
23.	group boxes	group boxes		
24.		pull-down lists		

Although you can find the detailed description of these user interface interaction components in the respective style guides, it is important to understand the recommended usage of these components in object-oriented GUI design (explained in the same order as in Table 9-1).

  1 Each GUI application features one or more primary windows containing the primary application objects. A primary window can be split into more than one window pane, each presenting a different part of the same document. Multiple windows, or multiple panels within a primary window, may be used to display the alternative views of an object. Different types of application objects may be presented in multiple primary windows or in multiple document windows contained in a multiple-document interface window as suggested in the Windows Interface design guide (Microsoft 1992) and the earlier version of SAA/CUA style guide (IBM 1989).

2 As secondary windows, dialog boxes may be used to present secondary application objects (e.g., file-selection dialog, font-selection dialog); to request user responses on the additional attribute settings of an object in a primary window object; to provide context-sensitive information; or to prompt for user instruction. Dialog boxes may have modal or modeless behavior. A modal dialog accepts user inputs only within the dialog window itself, and a modeless dialog allows user interactions with other application windows.

3 With the object-action interaction model, the primary windows contain the primary application objects, while the menu bar pull-down menus contain the actions for the objects. Possible choices of the different views of an object or the object attributes may also be presented as pull-down menu items. There are several guidelines for designing the menu bar.

- Use single words for menu-bar topics.
- Place menu-bar topics in a logical execution order.

Guidelines for pull-down menus include the following (Raap and Roske-Hofstrand 1988):

- Place the more frequently used choices near the top (e.g., File: New, Open, Close, Save).
- Show similar choices in logical groups separated by solid lines (e.g., Cut, Copy, Paste; Search, Replace).
- For choices that result in a dialog box (a secondary window), place ellipsis (...) following the choice (e.g., Open..., Search...).

Because users are most comfortable with a consistent environment, menu topics and pull-down choices should not change, except for choices unavailable in current context. In this case, set the choices insensitive (also called dimmed, disabled, or unavailable in different style guides). For example, **Paste** is insensitive, until after **Cut** (or **Copy**) action has taken effect.

4 The Apple desktop interface provides scrolling menus when there are too many menu items to fit into the height of the display screen. Other style guides use multiple-column menus to accommodate a large number of choice items. SAA/CUA recommends putting less than 10 items in a menu pane and using submenus to organize them into small chunks when the

number of items is large.

5 When many choice items are available, the menu items may be organized in separate groups. Each group has a title, while the choices of a group are displayed in a submenu. Although it is space-efficient, there is no visual cue to indicate the presence of submenu choice items until the main menu pane is pulled down.

6 When a single-valued attribute has a number of possible values, a pop-up menu may be used in Apple Desktop Interface. Only the current selection is displayed while the remaining choices are hidden until a user selects the associated button. A pop-up menu is space-efficient, while providing a visual cue to indicate its presence.

7 As a user works with a GUI application, it may be necessary to make menu selections repeatedly, which can be awkward if all the choices are in the menu-bar pull-downs. A pop-up menu has no visual cue to signify its presence, but, as it pops up right at the mouse pointer position, spatial context-sensitive action or choice items are made available to the user. This allows better user performance when it is compared with menu-bar pull-downs.

8 The tear-off menu in the Apple Desktop Interface, or the menu with push-pin in OPEN LOOK style, is a pull-down menu (or pop-up menu in row 7 of Table 9-1) pane that is left open. The user is allowed to place it anywhere on a display. Its visual presence and flexibility in placement allow efficient user interactions.

9 Mutually exclusive graphical choices may be used such as tool, color, or pattern palettes.

10 Push buttons present the actions in a window. Users expect immediate application response when they press a push button.

11 A check box displays a multivalued attribute or a list of object attributes that have true/false values. The user may select more than one item.

12 Radio buttons adopt the car-radio metaphor in which the user selects only one radio station. As one item is selected, every other item will be de-selected. Radio buttons are used to allow users to make a selection from a small number of possible values of an attribute. The radio buttons provide a strong visual cue for each of the items, but take more display space.

13 A spin button uses the metaphor of a mechanical spinning wheel that contains a range of fixed-increment values. It is used for selecting a value of an attribute from the full range of its possible fixed-increment values. The hour of a day, the day of a week, and the month of a year are all examples of such attributes. A spin button takes little display space and has a visual cue to indicate its presence.

14 Dials, sliders, or scales use the metaphor of their corresponding analog devices. They allow user selection from the full-range display of a continuous-valued attribute. They take a little more space than the spin button.

The application functional core can update the current value of an attribute when it is used as a progress indicator.

15 Scrollbars allow a user to scroll a large span of an object through a smaller viewing area. They are used in the primary windows to allow user control of the viewing area of interest. For attributes with a large number of possible choices, a scrollbar may also be used to limit the visible choices to less than 10 items.

16 A list may be used to display the member objects of a container object or the possible values of an object attribute. A scrollbar may be used together with a list to limit the number of visible items and the required display space if there are many items in the list.

17 The hierarchical scrolling list is specified only in the OPEN LOOK style guide. It is used to display a list of objects that have hierarchical relationships among them. A tree-structured file system and a class hierarchy are examples that might use such an interaction component.

18 A combination box combines an editable text field, and a list box. The text field displays either an item selected from the list or text entered by the user. The list box may contain the possible values of an attribute or the member objects of a container object.

19 The list box of a combination box occupies display space. To improve the space consumption, a drop-down combination box would not display the list box until a user presses the drop-down button.

20 Tables and matrices display their contents in a two-dimensional layout. A number of attributes of several objects may be presented together in a table. Database records and spreadsheets are examples that use this type of user interface interaction component.

21 Text fields may be either editable or read-only. They are used to get user textual input data or to display textual information.

22 Forms are composed of pairs of labels and text fields to present values of object attributes. This interaction component uses the familiar metaphor of a form. To compose user interface with style guides other than the NextStep Environment, this interaction component can easily be composed from labels and text fields.

23 Group boxes visually separate the settings of different attributes in a dialog box. Since a dialog box may contain the settings of several attributes presented as check boxes, radio buttons, or spin buttons, a group box confines each group of representation while it visually separates the attributes.

24 The NextStep pull-down list interaction component has similar behavior to the pull-down menus in row 3 in Table 9-1—to contain action items—but it has little use in the NextStep environment.

Although some of the empty cells in Table 9-1 can be filled in by composing new user interface interaction components from the existing ones, it is more important to be consistent with other applications in the same graphical environment than it is to create new interaction components that offer a confusing array of interaction styles.

In addition to style guides, the software vendors also offer the implementation of these user interface interaction components in the form of reusable software toolkits or application frameworks. A number of these reusable toolkits will be examined in Chapter 12.

9.5   USER INTERFACE DESIGN GUIDELINES

Before mapping an object model into a style-specific GUI design, we review general user interface design style guidelines. We also discuss design guidelines for designing GUIs to run on multiple graphical environments.

9.5.1   General Design Guidelines

There are many well-regarded guidelines in designing GUIs. They have evolved over the years from studies and practices in human-computer interaction. We present these guidelines in the context of object-oriented GUI design.

- **Arrange object-model information in users' scanning order.**
  Design the layout of application windows according to the users' natural scanning order. In Western-language-speaking countries, this order is from left to right and from top to bottom.
- **Arrange object-model information according to priority.**
  As discussed in Chapter 7, the usage pattern indicates the priority of object-model elements.

E X A M P L E   9 – 1

1   In a pull-down menu, the choice item on top has the highest priority.
2   Complying with the OSF/Motif style guide, push buttons at the bottom of dialog boxes are displayed from left to right. The **OK** button is used most frequently and should be on the left, followed by **Apply**, **Cancel**, and **Help** buttons.

- **Arrange object-model information to optimize user performance.**
  To optimize a user's performance, frequently accessed object-model elements should take minimum interaction steps and processing time. This principle helps us to choose the appropriate GUI interaction components to present the object models.

E X A M P L E   9 – 2

A frequently used control action positioned in a context-sensitive pop-up menu requires fewer interaction steps than it would positioned in a menu bar's pull-down menu. Instead of selecting the action in a menu pane that pops up right at the mouse pointer position, the latter arrangement would require a user to move the mouse pointer to the menu bar, select the appropriate title to pull down the menu pane, and traverse the mouse pointer to the choice item to make a selection.

- **Arrange similar object-model elements in groups.**
  As shown in Chapter 7, object-model elements are organized in groups. Grouping similar elements would put them into smaller, more discernible chunks.

9.5.2   Design Guidelines for Multiple Graphical Environments

A GUI design requirement of supporting multiple graphical environments may mean one of the following variations or some combination of these variations. Each of the variations also has its respective design guidelines.

Supporting Multiple GUI Style Guides. Vendor-specific style guides are the dominant graphical environment on their respective computing platforms. To reach a larger customer base, software developers may have to support multiple GUI styles.

The implication of this requirement is twofold. On one hand, to minimize implementation effort, it imposes constraints on user interface designers to use as many equivalent GUI interaction components as possible. On the other hand, to be competitive with similar products in the same graphical environment, a user interface designer needs to take full advantage of a specific style guide to select the best possible GUI interaction components for a design, risking the downside of increased implementation effort.

Guidelines

- **Use as many as possible equivalent GUI interaction components in different style guides.**
  Equivalent GUI interaction components are similar in appearance and behavior. The more of these that are used in a GUI design, the easier it is to implement the design in software.
- **Improve the design by using style-specific interaction components where necessary.**
  For certain specific situations, a style guide may offer a better selection of GUI interaction components that have no equivalent counterparts in other style guides. For example, the pop-up menu specified in the SAA/CUA, OSF/Motif, and OPEN LOOK style guides are highly context-sensitive and space-efficient, although there is no equivalent interaction component in the Apple Desktop Interface, or the NextStep style guides.

Supporting multiple locales. A native language is the dominant language in every country, just as native sociocultural phenomena are unique to each region. Designing an application to support multiple locales allows that application to reach a larger customer base.

The implication of multiple-locale support may result in a very different GUI presentation design, especially when the languages involved have a different scanning order (e.g., English versus Hebrew) or characters (e.g., English alphabet versus Chinese ideogram). We will also have to examine the source metaphor of an application to see if it is experiential for the different cultures.

Guidelines

- **Use a culturally neutral source metaphor if it exists.**
  The source metaphor must be experiential, as we have shown in Chapter 8. A well-matched source metaphor for one culture may not have the same conceptual bearings for another. However, different metaphors require additional effort in implementation. A culturally neutral metaphor would minimize such effort.
- **Use culturally neutral graphical representation when possible.**
  Graphical elements in user interface designs require a lot of effort to develop. The icon images, pointer shapes, or bitmaps must reflect the source metaphor and convey the same meaning to users from different target cultures.

9.6   PRESENTING APPLICATION OBJECTS

In Chapter 6, we saw that the object modeling of an application identifies objects; the relationships among them; their attributes, operations, alternative views; and the facets of attributes. In Chapter 7, we established the priority of classes of application objects and the relationships among them. In Chapter 8, we selected a source metaphor to represent the object model. In this section, we concentrate on presenting objects in a GUI design.

Regardless of the differences among various user interface styles, any style-specific user interface design would be guided by the same high-level abstraction of an object model. The following guidelines are used when presenting application objects.

- **Present each class of the application objects in separate windows.**
  Each application object is characterized by a set of relationships, alternative views, operations, attributes, and the attributes facets. If each window contains only one class of application objects, the associated actions are organized according to their priority and grouping as menu items, or control panel items. Users will not get confused about which actions can be applied to which objects.

- **Present each aggregation or container object in separate windows.**
  As we have presented in Chapter 6, an aggregation class contains other classes and a container class contains member objects of the same class. An aggregation class may be nested to contain other aggregation classes. These classes are often the centerpiece of an application (e.g., the document class in a desktop publishing application, the drawing class in a drawing application), and therefore should be presented in the primary windows.

- **Present application objects with their respective metaphorical representation.**
  In the metaphor selection process examined in Chapter 8, the application objects and the structural relationships among them were the key matching criteria. Since the application objects are the focus of users' attention in their application sessions, the metaphor of an application is best conveyed through them.

- **Present the primary application objects in the primary windows.**
  Application objects are the focus of attention throughout a user's application session. The primary application objects are frequently interacted with and must be readily accessible. Since each of the application objects has a set of associated actions, it should be presented in its own individual window. Each of the user interface styles we examined in the last section offers similar primary windows representation. The multiple-document interface (MDI) defined in the Windows Interface design guide (Microsoft 1992) and the earlier SAA/CUA specification (IBM 1989) offers a single primary window which contains multiple "document windows" displaying a number of application objects.

E X A M P L E   9 – 3

An application has two primary application objects. In Figure 9-2, these objects are presented in two primary windows.

- **Present the alternative views of an application object in a single window with single or multiple document windows (or panels)**.
  Depending on the application object, we can present a number of alternative views to emphasize different aspects of an application object. For example, we can present data files as items in a list, as icons in a workspace, or as opened files in separate document windows. We can also display alternative views of the same object simultaneously in the separate panels (or window panes) of a primary window. For example, applications like a file browser, an electronic bulletin-board news reader, or an electronic mail can present the list of items in one panel and the content of one item in another panel. In Figure 9-3, two views of a file-system object are presented in two panels of a document window in the multiple document interface.

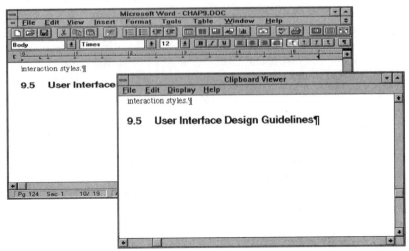

Figure 9-2. Two primary classes are presented as two primary windows.

- **Present secondary application object classes in the secondary windows.**

  Secondary application classes are less frequently accessed during a user's application session. We can present them in secondary windows to be popped up only when needed. In the example of the *ftp* program, the remote-host object is only accessed when establishing a connection. Since it is less frequently used, we can present this application object in the secondary window. In Figure 9-4, a secondary application object is presented in a secondary window.

9.7 PRESENTING RELATIONSHIPS

As application objects are presented in separate windows, visually representing the dynamic relationships among the windows of application objects is often a challenge. Lacking good visual representations, the relationships among the application objects' windows are usually implicitly implied. The following common practices in GUI designs demonstrate the implicit nature of representing relationships.

1 Two primary windows containing two related classes may not be apparent to the user unless some action taken in one window updates the information displayed in another window (see Figure 9-5).

2 The relationship between a primary window and a pop-up secondary window becomes apparent only after the secondary window is popped up by a user selecting a pull-down menu item.

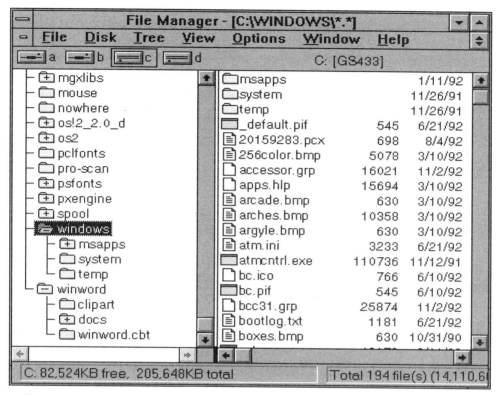

Figure 9–3. Alternative views of an application object are presented in two panels of a document window.

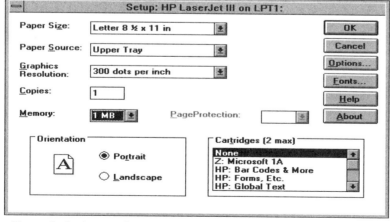

Figure 9–4. A secondary application object is presented in a secondary window.

3 Although the drag-and-drop interaction is allowed between two objects that are related, a user may not be aware of the existing relationship until a visual cue is displayed when a source object is dragged over some legal target object (see Figure 9-6).

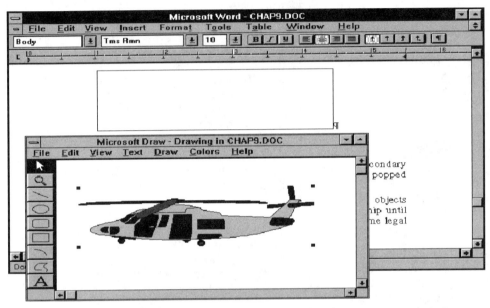

Figure 9–5. Two related application objects are presented in two primary windows.

Figure 9–6. Drag-and-drop between two related container objects.

9.8   PRESENTING OPERATIONS, ATTRIBUTES, AND FACETS

Because of human cognitive consideration and display space limitation, all elements of an object model must be prioritized and grouped, and then presented in order according to their priority and grouping. In Chapter 7, the user interface system-level design involved the activities of prioritizing and grouping object-model elements. So far in this chapter, we have already examined the presentation of application objects and their relationships. The alternative views of an object can be selected by a user from a **View** menu-bar title. The secondary object window can be popped up from selecting a pull-down menu item.

In this section, we examine the presentation of the remaining object-model elements, namely, the operations, attributes, and their facets.

9.8.1   Presenting Operations

An operation results in immediate application action that queries or changes the attributes of an object. High-priority operations are those more frequently used by users, and therefore they should be quickly accessible. Lower-priority operations must still be accessible, but a user may have to take more navigation steps to access them. We can use the following user interface interaction components to present an operation.

Push Buttons in a Primary-Window Control Panel. High-priority operations may be laid out as push buttons in a control panel (or in *toolbar* as seen in many new applications running on Microsoft® Windows™ 3.x environment). Figure 9-7 shows such an example.

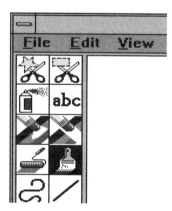

Figure 9–7.   Control panel in the Microsoft® Paintbrush application.

Pulldown or Pop-up Menu Items. Operations are most often arranged as choice items in menu panes. The higher priority items may use a context-sensitive pop-up menu (row 7 in Table 9-1). In each menu pane, higher priority operations are positioned near the top.

9.8.2   Presenting Object Attributes

An user accesses the attributes of an application object to perform two types of actions: to query or to modify the object state. Depending on the priority of attributes and their grouping and the facets of an attribute, there are a number of ways to present attributes.

Attribute Palettes in the Primary Windows. The paragraph alignment in a word processing application or the foreground/background color in a drawing application are high-priority attributes. They may be laid out explicitly in the primary window area to allow easy access. In Figure 9-8, the color attribute is presented as a color palette in a primary window.

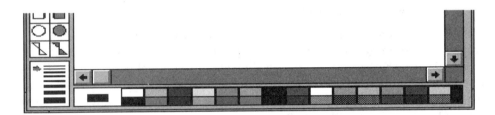

Figure 9–8. Color palette in the Microsoft Paintbrush application.

Attribute Group Boxes in the Secondary Windows. Depending on the facets of an attribute, a group box may contain check boxes for multi-valued attribute, radio buttons for single-valued attribute, a list for either single-valued or multivalued attribute, or a matrix for multiple attributes with the same facets (e.g., the possible values of read, write, and execute for the attributes of owner, group, and world accesses in a UNIX file object).

9.8.3 Presenting Attribute Facets

The facets of an attribute include its default value, data type, accessibility, and possible values. A user shouldn't have to memorize all the possible values of an attribute to perform a task—that would slow down task performance, and it is highly error prone. Depending on the data type and the range of the possible values of an attribute, there are several ways to present the facets.

- **Pop-up menu (row 6 in Table 9-1):** used when an attribute has a small number of possible values (less than 10), and the display space is limited.
- **Spin button (row 13 in Table 9-1):** used when the attribute has fixed-increment values, and display space is limited.
- **Radio buttons (row 12 in Table 9-1):** used when there are only three or four possible values and there is available display space. They provide strong visual cues for all possible values.
- **Check box (row 11 in Table 9-1):** used when there is a multivalued attribute or a number of attributes that have Boolean (true or false) values.
- **Slider (row 14 in Table 9-1):** used when the possible values fall anywhere between an upper and a lower limit.

- **List boxes (row 16 in Table 9-1):** present strong visual cue for visible list items. A scrolling list may contain a large number of possible values of an attribute. A user may quickly scroll through the list to find the desired item. It does occupy some space, but a scrolling list should display no more than 10 visible items.

- **Palettes (row 9 in Table 9-1):** used when some type of facets are best represented graphically, such as icons, bitmaps, colors, and other graphical symbols. Palettes may be presented in a primary or secondary window or in a pull-down menu that can be torn-off (row 8 in Table 9-1).

- **Text fields (row 21 in Table 9-1):** Used as a last resort when a user needs to specify the value of an attribute. It is easy for a user to make mistakes and require exact memory recall of an attribute value.

9.9 SUMMARY

In this chapter, we have presented object-oriented GUI design that maps a user interface-level object model to style-specific GUI designs. We went beyond the look-and-feel differences of the GUI interaction components specified in various style guides.

We identified common interaction models. We then examined GUI interaction components from a number of vendor-specific user interface style guides to list all the similar interaction components. Next we discussed the style-specific GUI design process as a simple process of identifying appropriate user interface interaction components to represent the user interface-level object model. The object-model elements of objects, relationships, alternative views, operations, attributes, and attribute facets are all mapped to style-specific user interface designs.

9.10 BIBLIOGRAPHIC NOTES

In various published user interface design style guidelines (Apple Computer 1987, 1991; IBM 1991a, 1991b; Microsoft 1992; Open Software Foundation 1990a; Sun Microsystems 1990), you can find descriptions of general user interface design principles and style-specific GUI interaction components. Although these publications do not specifically address the object-oriented GUI design approach as we have presented it in this book, they do provide a more detailed description of various user interface interaction components and examples of their usage.

CHAPTER 10

Contextual Graphical User Interface Design

*I*n the previous chapter, the object-oriented GUI design focused on mapping the user interface-level object model. In this chapter, we present contextual GUI design, which informs the users of their current context throughout their application session.

In GUI design, modes are sometimes necessary to restrict user's interaction with the application. The traditional character-based user interface design in a nonwindowing environment could display only a screen-full of information at a time. Its restrictive sequences of screen displays result in strong temporal modes. In contrast, an object-oriented GUI design in a windowing environment displays several windows of application-object information simultaneously. Although temporal modes are less common in object-oriented GUIs, spatial modes are commonly found because users can maintain only one focus of attention at a time on an application, as limited by human task-performance ability.

Context-sensitive GUI provides visual cues and contextual messages to guide users throughout their application sessions. Visual cues are graphical information reflecting current context with specific cursor shapes, highlighting, or shades of color. Contextual messages offer status, information, warning, confirmation, error, and help messages specific to current context.

10.1 STATES AND THEIR DEPENDENCIES IN GUI

As users proceed in their application sessions to perform their tasks, they move through states of different circumstances. There may also be dependencies among these states, such that only certain sequences of actions are allowed to go from one state to another. The challenge in GUI design is to inform users of the state they are in at any given time and to convey the dependencies that may exist among these states. Let's examine these two issues further.

10.1.1 Informing Current State

Object-oriented GUI applications present well-organized object-model information to the users. Each application object has a number of attributes to characterize it. In this approach of GUI design, there are methods of informing users of their current state.

Visually Present the Application Object's Views Reflecting Its Current Attribute Values. With some appropriate source-metaphor mapping, the multiple views of an object should closely reflect the current values of its attributes.

E X A M P L E   1 0 – 1

Many desktop publishing applications have the feature of so-called WYSIWYG (what you see is what you get) that presents the document object to match closely with the actual hard-copy output. The attributes of fonts, graphics, and document layout are displayed that closely reflect their current values.

Provide Contextual Information. Visual presentation reflects current state but not how users reached the current state or what the alternatives are in moving on to the next state. Contextual information in the form of status messages, information messages, or help messages informs the user about the current state and alternative paths with more descriptive information. Well-designed contextual information would explain the current task, its preconditions and postconditions, and upcoming tasks.

10.1.2 Conveying State Dependencies

Because of the nature of each application, it is inevitable to have state dependencies in many applications. However, without an appropriate source metaphor to reflect the state dependencies, users of various skill levels may have a hard time recognizing them. Therefore, the best solution is to devise a source metaphor that can convey any target-application state dependency to the users.

With object-oriented GUI design, state dependencies exist in the system-level (dynamic relationships among the application objects), as well as in the object-level (state transitions among its operations). Let's examine these two cases in more depth.

State Dependencies Among Application Objects. In Chapter 8, the metaphor-mapping process focused on the application objects and the structural relationships among them. A source metaphor selected by following the guidelines should also reflect the state dependency among the application objects.

E X A M P L E 1 0 – 2

The file transfer program (ftp) has a number of state dependencies that are clearly conveyed with the *file-repository* metaphor, as shown in Table 10-1.

Table 10–1 State Dependencies of the ftp Application and Its Source Metaphor

ftp Application	*File-Repository* Metaphor
A remote host must be accessible before transferring files.	A file repository must be accessible in order to put/get files.
To get a file, a user must change to the directory containing the file.	To retrieve a file, a user must open the drawer that stores the file.

State Dependencies Among the Operations of an Application Object. An application object may have the typical operations of create, destroy, cut, copy, and paste. There are the obvious state dependencies: An object must be created before it can be destroyed; an object must be cut or copied before it can be pasted.

In order to convey state dependencies to users, contextual GUI design offers visual cues and contextual messages, which we will discuss later in this chapter.

10.2 TEMPORAL AND SPATIAL MODES

Modes are introduced during user interface design to restrict users' interaction with the application. They arise from various constraints in the computing environment, the application, and the users' cognitive capacity. In GUI design, it is common to have spatial modes and temporal modes.

Temporal modes arise from computation-environment limitations, such that the application information has to be displayed in some sequence rather than simultaneously. Temporal modes demand more cognitive load from the users to memorize previously displayed information and the specific steps to invoke commands.

In contrast, users can freely switch among several windows in a graphical environment. The different windows and the different areas of a window may only allow certain user actions, which is defined as spatial modes (Thimbleby 1990). However, due to inherent human performance limitations, users focus their attention on only a small area on a display screen at a time. Visual cues must be provided to help users locate a specific spatial mode and focus their attention on a display area.

10.2.1 Temporal Modes

In traditional user interface applications, the limited desktop computing power, graphics software, display and input-device technologies placed many constraints on the user interface design. Not that long ago, an "interactive" application would present one screen of information at a time to prompt for user input. To perform a certain action, a user might have to go step-by-step from one screen to the next until reaching the screen containing the desired selection. This kind of user interface design has many temporal modes. The highly sequential arrangement of screens offers little flexibility for user actions. The memory load required of a user is very large with even simple applications.

Temporal modes impose heavy sequential ordering among each screen of information display, and yet they may not be obvious at all to users. The dialog-oriented rather than object-oriented style also results in more sequential ordering that makes the user interface very rigid.

With object-oriented GUI in a windowing environment, the sequential ordering among information displays is minimized, but the temporal modes still exist in the form of unavailable information and secondary windows (modal dialog boxes). However, in such a windowing environment, contextual status messages and help messages may be provided to guide the users.

10.2.2 Spatial Modes

Spatial modes are the current context of input action throughout users' application sessions. A user can focus on only one display area at a time to perform input actions. In a windowing environment, several application objects may be displayed simultaneously along with a large amount of graphical/textual information. Spatial modes are common in such an environment to limit a user's input action to one area at a time.

With spatial modes, users can freely access many display elements and switch among them easily with a pointing device. In this case, users need assistance from the application to find the display element of interest, to focus their attention, and to perform a specific action. Visual cues in the form of highlighting a display element, changing the pointer shape, and other visual feedback would help users to perform these tasks. Contextual messages also provide users with information of current mode and how to proceed in their application session.

10.3 VISUAL CUES IN VARIOUS STYLE GUIDES

Since many modes, including spatial modes and some temporal modes, exist in GUIs, we must provide visual cues to help the user recognize the current mode and perform visual search of graphical elements. Similar to our discussion in Chapter 9, every vendor-specific GUI style guide defines a number of visual cues to inform users of modes. The following sections present the common visual cues of pointer and cursor shapes, color-coded access modes, highlighted display elements, and dimmed controls.

10.3.1 Pointers and Cursors

In GUIs, a pointer indicates the current position of a pointing device (e.g., a mouse, a tablet), and a cursor indicates the current position of a keyboard device. Both pointers and cursors are essential indicators of the spatial modes in GUIs. They change shape according to the specific spatial mode they are in. In the mode that results from a long computing operation when no user input is accepted, the application also changes the pointer to a busy pointer shape.

10.3.2 Color-Coded Access Modes

A GUI may present information that is read-only, selectable, or modifiable by the user. To help users differentiate the access mode of displayed information, the information display area background may be color coded with an appropriate background color (see Figure 10-1).

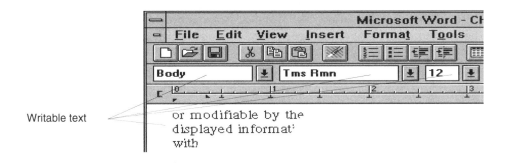

Figure 10–1. Color-coded access mode of object attributes.

10.3.3 Highlighted Active Objects and Action

There may be a number of windows displayed simultaneously in a GUI application, each containing many of their respective actions. We must provide visual highlighting to help users focus their attention on the active object(s) and action. In Figure 10-2, the active object (the 3.5˝diskette) is highlighted with resize handles around it, and the selected **Cut** action is highlighted with dark background.

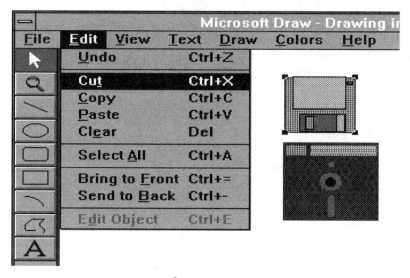

Figure 10–2. In a Microsoft® Draw session, the 3.5´´ diskette is the active object to receive the selected **Cut** action.

10.3.4 Highlighted Default Actions

When we use control buttons to present the actions of an object, we can assign one of the more frequently taken actions as the default action. When a default action is present, a user can hit the Enter key (or Return key in some other keyboard standards) to apply the default action to the selected object(s). A default button has specific visual cues to differentiate itself from other push-button controls. In Figure 10-3, the **Yes** button is highlighted with heavy border indicating it as the default action.

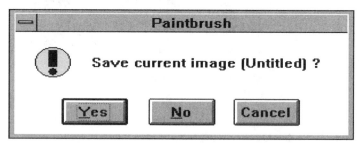

Figure 10–3. The **Yes** button is the default action highlighted with heavy border.

10.3.5 Highlighted Active Attribute Values

Each object attribute has its associated facets. There may be many possible values for an attribute. A default value or currently selected value is highlighted as the active value of an attribute. Figure 10-4 shows an example with such highlighted active attribute values.

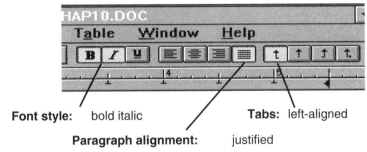

Figure 10–4. The "ribbon" area located below the menu bar displays the active attribute values of font style, paragraph alignment, and tabs in a Microsoft® Word For Windows session.

10.3.6 Dimmed Unavailable Actions

One type of mode exists in GUIs due to various state dependencies in the underlying application. As discussed in the first section of this chapter, there may be state dependencies at the system level among the application objects or at the object level among the operations. When the precondition state is not fulfilled, a number of actions may be inactive and unavailable to the user. In this case, a dimmed foreground is used as a visual cue to inform users of the unavailable actions. In Figure 10-2, the pull-down menu item **Edit Object** is a dimmed unavailable action.

10.4 CONTEXTUAL MESSAGES IN STYLE GUIDES

Contextual messages provide mostly textual information to help users realize their current state in much more detail than visual cues. Different types of contextual messages can offer different levels of detail. Status messages provide concise descriptions for both user interface modes and application states. Help messages can be more descriptive to inform the overall spatial- or temporal-mode contexts and to instruct on how to proceed in some dependent states. Information, warning, and error messages are contextual messages presented in dialog boxes.

10.4.1 Status Messages

Status messages are short and concise textual descriptions and are a very effective contextual information source for both novice and experienced users. They are recommended as Help Balloons in Apple Desktop Interface (Apple Computer 1991), as information areas and status areas in SAA/CUA (IBM 1991a, 1991b), as message bars and status bars in Windows Interface (Microsoft 1992), and as footer messages in OPEN LOOK (Sun Microsystems 1990). Their usage is summarized as follows:

- **For contextual messages in general:** Status messages are space-efficient and provide strong visual cues. With short and concise messages, the status message may be popped up as contextual help balloons (Apple Computer 1991) or placed as a one-line header or footer text field of any primary window (Microsoft 1992; IBM 1991a; Sun Microsystems 1990) or secondary window (Sun Microsystems 1990).

- **For mode messages:** Status messages explain spatial mode (e.g., the usage of a selected menu item), inform users of temporal mode (e.g., current page number in a long document) or other type of mode (e.g., selected certain drawing tool in a drawing application).

- **For current state messages:** Status messages inform on the current state (e.g., computation in progress; operation is completed) and what to do next.

In the SAA/CUA style guide, the global status messages for all member objects in a container object are displayed in a primary window's header area called *status area*, and both the state and mode messages may be displayed in a window's footer area called *information area*.

In the Windows Interface design guide, a message bar is placed at the bottom of the window to display state and mode messages. A status bar is a subdivided message bar which simultaneously displays information for several modes (e.g., keyboard mode, current pointer position). In Figure 10-5, we show an example of a status bar.

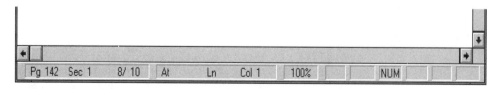

Figure 10–5. Status-message area provides contextual information.

In OPEN LOOK style guidelines, both state and mode messages are displayed in the footer area of primary or secondary windows. The left side of the footer is for error messages and short-term messages, which include progress, completion, and instruction messages—mostly state messages in our definition. The right side of the footer is for medium-term messages, mostly mode messages in our definition.

10.4.2 Information, Warning, and Error-Message Dialogs

Information, warning, and error-message dialogs are state messages displayed in a popup dialog window as a result of an application entering abnormal state. They require response from the user to be closed. These messages are also concise as in status messages. With their center-stage positioning, additional visual cues, and modal behavior, they draw immediate attention from the users.

10.4.3 Help Messages

We can divide help messages into several categories. In the Help menu-bar pull-down, the categories of help index and tutorial are common in many style guides. As context-sensitive help messages, they are displayed in a separate window in response to users pressing the Help key on a keyboard or the Help button in dialog boxes.

Help on Context. Context-sensitive help describes specific actions and how the user can use them. The help description can be for spatial modes that are field by field and action by action.

Help on Window. This gives information about the current window's functions and tasks that can be performed.

Help on Keys. Function keys, accelerator keys, and other special use of keys assigned by the application are described.

Help Index. This provides an alphabetical list of available help topics.

Help Tutorial. Complex applications can provide an on-line help tutorial to guide users through a typical task scenario.

10.5 SUMMARY

In this chapter, we have presented the contextual GUI design that informs users of their current status throughout their application sessions. State dependencies inherent in most applications require an application to provide clear direction to users. Spatial mode and temporal mode are two other examples requiring contextual GUI design effort.

By using visual cues, status messages, context-sensitive help messages, and other forms of contextual GUI design, users will be informed of the state and mode they are in during an application session.

This completes the GUI design activity. In the next chapter, we will discuss the software architectural design of GUI applications and the mapping of object-oriented and contextual GUI designs into software implementation.

10.6 BIBLIOGRAPHIC NOTES

The same GUI style guides we have mentioned in the previous chapter also describe various style-specific ways to provide contextual information to users (Apple Computer 1987, 1991; IBM 1991a, 1991b; Microsoft 1992; Open Software Foundation 1990a; Sun Microsystems 1990). You can find many examples of contextual GUI design in these publications.

GRAPHICAL USER INTERFACE SOFTWARE IMPLEMENTATION

C H A P T E R **11**

Software Architectural Design of Graphical User Interface Applications

*I*n chapters 9 and 10, we examined the two important aspects of GUI design, namely the object-oriented and contextual aspects. In this chapter, we discuss the software architectural design of GUI applications.

Software architectural design deals with the modular partitioning and interfacing the modules of an application. The major architectural design objective is to map the object-oriented and contextual GUI design to some optimal software subsystems and subsystem-interfacing mechanisms. The architectural design also considers the application functional subsystem, which provides application-specific computations.

11.1 Decomposing a Software System

The software system-modeling approach partitions a software system into smaller logical subsystems. Depending on the system-modeling approach and the characteristics of an application, the partitioning criteria may vary, resulting in very different configurations. In the next sections, we consider the basic system-modeling approaches and the various application-specific configurations that may result by combining the basic partitioning approach in different ways.

11.1.1 Basic Software-System Decomposition Approaches

To manage the complexity of software-system design, a number of decomposition approaches have evolved over the years, each with their respective emphasis on different aspects of the problem at hand.

Functional Decomposition. Functional decomposition emphasizes decomposing the processing steps of application functions. In its early development, the rigid approach of hierarchical decomposition ended with many duplicating functional modules.

Data-Flow Decomposition. By concentrating on the flow of data throughout a software system, we can partition that software system into processes, flows, data stores, and terminators (Yourdon 1989). Although it may not seem intuitive to consider the data flow in a system, the functional processes that transform data inputs to outputs are really the focus of this decomposition approach.

If we compare this with the functional decomposition, we can see that the improvement lies in the addition of data into the picture that connects the functional processes.

Entity-Relationship Decomposition. Further along in the decomposition evolution, the entity-relationship model (Chen 1976) puts even more emphasis on the data, along with the relationships among data stores, to provide a network model of a software system. An entity-relationship model consists of object types, attributes, relationships, associate object types, and supertypes/subtypes (Teorey, Yang, and Fry 1986; Shlaer and Mellor 1988; Yourdon 1989). The entity-relationship model describes the data aspects of a real-world problem in its high-level abstraction.

Object-Oriented Decomposition. The development in knowledge representation (Minsky 1975) and entity-relationship model (Chen 1976) preceded the next evolutionary step of the object-oriented approach (Booch 1991; Coad and Yourdon 1991; Rumbaugh et al. 1991; Shlaer and Mellor 1992). Object-oriented decomposition uses the added notion of classes that encapsulates both the data (attributes) and their respective functional processes (operations) and class inheritance that generalizes/specializes classes into a class hierarchy.

11.1.2 Layers of Software Abstractions

Application software may use services provided by the operating system, the windowing environment, the network management system, or the database management system. Directly interfacing with these system services creates rigid dependencies to a specific system configuration. Implementing layers of abstraction between the application software and the underlying system services results in more flexible and portable application configuration.

Reusable user interface toolkits are usually implemented with layers of abstractions. The bottom layer interfaces with the low-level graphics drawing, window-manipulation function calls. The higher layers may provide GUI interaction-component classes and event-handling mechanisms.

11.2 SUBSYSTEMS INTERFACING MECHANISMS

The subsystems based on any of the decomposition models are all interconnected in some fashion. The significance of these interconnections is their run-time realization of dynamic behavior among the subsystems. Each of the basic partitioning approaches in the last section may employ more than one interfacing mechanism. The application-specific configuration may also have to incorporate different interfacing mechanisms to provide an optimal solution.

11.2.1 Basic Interfacing Mechanisms

We can use a number of basic interfacing mechanisms to realize the interconnection of subsystems.

Sequential Procedural Call. Procedural calls invoke functional processes—input data is transformed in the procedure to produce output. All decomposition models may use this mechanism as part of their implementation, but the emphasis varies. It implies state or data-flow dependencies between the calling procedure and the procedure that is being called. Figure 11-1 illustrates the interfacing mechanism of procedural calls.

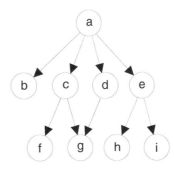

Figure 11–1. The interfacing mechanism of procedural calls.

Message Passing. Message passing uses messages to establish run-time connections. Although the mechanism itself may be implemented as procedural calls, the notion of a message implies low-bandwidth communication between subsystems. The message passing may also be bidirectional and, therefore, has less state or data-flow dependencies as in the directional procedural calls (see Figure 11-2).

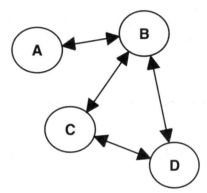

Figure 11–2. The message-passing interfacing mechanism among the subsystems of a large software system.

Event Responses. An event-responses mechanism uses a dispatching mechanism to invoke responses as it receives specific incoming events from other modules (see Figure 11-3). The event-responses mechanism allows asynchronous behavior among the software modules. As the individual response functions are registered with the dispatching mechanism, they do not have the state dependencies among them. This stateless nature allows modeless behavior in the software implementation of the GUI module.

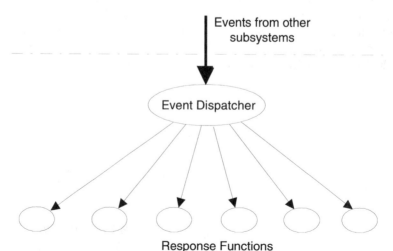

Figure 11–3. The event-responses interfacing mechanism.

11.2.2 Application-Specific Interfacing Configurations

Depending on the specific application, its actual implementation may employ all three of the interfacing mechanisms. As we will discuss in the following sections, in GUI applications, an event-responses mechanism dispatches user inputs to corresponding response functions. The response functions may call other sequential procedural calls to perform more computation within the GUI software module, use message-passing mechanisms to invoke further processing in the application functional core, or send display request messages to the window system module (see Figure 11-4).

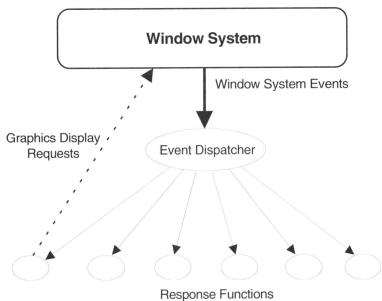

Figure 11–4. The interfacing mechanism of event-responses in a graphical environment.

11.3 DIALOG-INDEPENDENT SOFTWARE ARCHITECTURE

Dialog-independent user interface application software architecture (Hartson and Hix 1989; Myers 1991) divides software into a subsystem processing only the human-computer interactions and another subsystem processing only application functional core. Dialog-independent software architecture allows separate evolutionary refinement of user interfaces, as well as ease of maintenance.

The notion of dialog independence has been applied in GUIs in various forms of implementation. Smalltalk-80 introduced the model-view-controller (MVC) model (Krasner and Pope 1988), where models are the application function layer; views are the user interface presentation layer; and controllers handle user input-device interactions. A user interface implemented with OSF/Motif user interface language (UIL) (Open Software Foundation 1991b) separates form (GUI subsystem) from function (application functional core subsystem). In Inter-Views (Linton, Vlissides, and Calder 1989), there is the separation of view (interactive objects) and subject (abstract application behavior).

Dialog-independent software architecture may be extended to consider additional development requirements. The object-oriented GUI presented in this book has its unique characteristics to be considered in its architectural design, as we will see in the rest of this chapter. The following sections review some variations of dialog-independent GUI software architectures.

11.3.1 Model-View-Controller Software Architecture

MVC may be the earliest realization of an object-oriented dialog-independent software architecture (Krasner and Pope 1988). Many variations based on the MVC model have been proposed (e.g., Shan 1990). The MVC model consists of the decomposed components of model, view, and controllers; and the interfacing mechanism of message passing to broadcast changes to its dependents (see Figure 11-5).

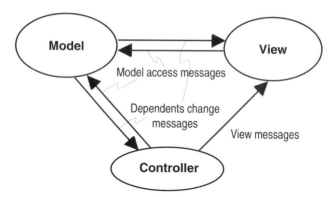

Figure 11–5. The model-view-controller architecture in Smalltalk-80.

Models. The models subsystem implements application functions that handle data-flow computation in response to user interaction sent from the controller component.

Views. Views include the graphical display of user interface layout and interactor views. The interactor views present GUI interaction objects (i.e., push buttons, lists, check boxes, etc.). Views also display data from the models components. A top-level view is the root of a view hierarchy. A superview does graphical transformation, windowing, and clipping between levels of the superview/subview hierarchy (see Figure 11-6).

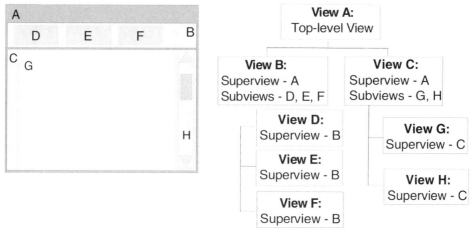

Figure 11–6. The view hierarchy of a GUI.

Controllers. Messages are sent to the model, and provide the interface between the model with its associated views and interactive user input devices (e.g., keyboard, mouse). Controllers also handle scheduling of interactions with other view-controller pairs. Menus can be thought of as view-controller pairs—they are considered as input devices and as controllers in Smalltalk.

Broadcasting Change. As a controller subsystem accepts user input actions, it sends messages to the model component to trigger a change. The change message is then broadcast to its controllers and views.

Dependents. Views and controllers associated with a model are registered as dependents of the model. They receive broadcasting messages whenever some aspects of a model are changed.

11.3.2 Event-Driven MVC Architecture

We can modify the MVC architecture in Smalltalk-80 and apply it to GUI application development in other graphical environments. As all the de facto standard graphical environments support event-handling mechanisms for user input device interactions, the definition of the architectural elements of controllers subsystem and subsystem-interfacing mechanisms should be adjusted accordingly.

In an event-driven MVC architecture, the controllers component becomes the event handler that dispatches user input-device events, windowing-environment events, and any other system events to the corresponding response functions in the models component. The models component also registers response functions with the controllers component.

11.4 Software Mapping of the Object-Oriented Design

The object-oriented GUI design presented in Chapter 9 maps the object model and its source metaphor into windows and other GUI components. Object-oriented GUI design maps the object-model elements of classes, dynamic relationships, operations, attributes, and attribute facets. The GUI presentation of each of the object elements interfaces with corresponding application functional core subsystem. The classes and the dynamic relationships among them are respectively the decomposed subsystems and the interfaces among them.

11.4.1 Software Mapping of Classes

Classes are the decomposed software modules. The software design of each class involves its individual subsystems of GUI and application functional core.

- With the object model as its underlying configuration, it is natural to partition the implementation software based on individual classes. Considering the requirements of platform independence and locale independence, we further separate out the GUI portion in each class as a subsystem.
- To implement the GUI subsystem, each class is presented in a primary or secondary window. Within each window, the software composition may also be subdivided into the areas of menu bar, workspace, control palettes, and so on (see Figure 11-6). A hierarchical composition of windows and its subwindows allows more flexible GUI presentation redesign, which is frequent in the evolutionary development life cycle.
- The presentation of alternative views of a class requires interfacing with application functional core subsystem. As a user action makes a selection of a specific view, an event-dispatching mechanism invokes the application functional core subsystem to generate the requested view through some other mechanism to the GUI environment.

11.4.2 Software Mapping of Dynamic Relationships

Dynamic relationships are the connections among the objects. As discussed in Chapter 9, the user realizes dynamic relationships as secondary windows are popped up, or as the drag-and-drop action is effected between a source object and a target object. These dynamic relationships are initiated by user actions and therefore suggest an event driven-mechanism to dispatch the specific event.

11.4.3 Software Mapping of Operations

Operations of a class are the user actions that change the values of its attributes. The users initiate an action by selecting it from the GUI presentation. The action invokes the corresponding application function to fetch or change the values of affected attributes. An event-responses interfacing mechanism is also necessary to dispatch these user actions to the application functional core subsystem, which performs the specific computation.

11.4.4 Software Mapping of Attributes and Their Facets

The user action of selecting an attribute value from the presented facets invokes the application functional core subsystem to change the value of an attribute. An event-responses interfacing mechanism would be very effective in dispatching such user actions.

The presentation of facets relies on the application function component to provide the up-to-date values. An interfacing mechanism must also be provided to transfer such information from the application function component to the presentation component.

11.5 SOFTWARE MAPPING OF THE CONTEXTUAL GUI DESIGN

As discussed in Chapter 10, contextual GUI design may be divided into mode-related and state-related aspects. Mode-related contextual design provides visual cues and contextual messages in response to user actions. State-related contextual design provides visual cues and contextual messages in response to an application's internal state transitions.

11.5.1 Modes

Modes are introduced in object-oriented GUI design to meet various constraints. During a user's application session, modes appear in response to user's actions. The contextual GUI design of visual cues and contextual messages are presented in response to such user actions (Figure 11-7).

There are several factors to consider in designing a software architecture to handle modes.

- Since a mode-related contextual GUI design responds to user actions, an event-responses interfacing mechanism should be used in each class implementation to handle modes.
- A mode also has its corresponding display element in the GUI presentation that accepts specific user input events, so there is a close association between the mode-related interfacing mechanism and the object-oriented GUI presentation.

11.5.2 States

State-related contextual GUI are provided as the software system goes through internal state changes. Because of state dependencies, user actions are restricted as the software system enters certain states. The software design to provide visual cues and contextual messages is similar to mode-related contextual design.

- To restrict user actions when there are state dependencies, the application

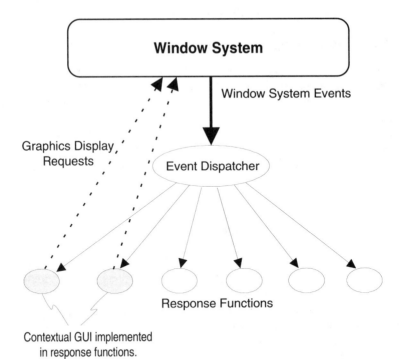

Figure 11–7. Contextual GUI design is implemented as part of the response functions.

functional core will have to instruct the event-dispatcher to limit the user input events that can be processed by the response functions.

- To present state-related contextual information to the users, the application functional core subsystem will have to pass messages to the GUI subsystem.

11.6 INTEGRATING THE APPLICATION

In the various architectural design considerations presented in the previous sections, we have constantly referred to the subsystems of the application functional core, the user interface, and the user interaction handling. Every basic interfacing mechanism may be employed to solve some specific problem. There are several additional considerations in integrating the various components of all the application classes.

- The major purpose of a GUI is to provide computation results in response to user actions. An interfacing mechanism must be designed to send the application output to the presentation component, which displays the output graphically.
- We may have to map a large aggregation class into a combination of more

than one primary windows, and secondary windows. These primary and secondary windows are all interconnected with data flows among them.

11.7 STYLE-INDEPENDENT SOFTWARE ARCHITECTURE

In Chapter 9, we examined a number of GUI style guides to map the application object model. User interface designers select appropriate GUI interaction components specified by the individual style guide to map an object model.

Although each style guide offers a different set of GUI interaction components, the intended usage and the actual function of individual components are very similar. The SAA/CUA and the OPEN LOOK styles seem to offer more choices of these components for specific needs of a user interface designer. All user interface style guides offer sufficient support for the comprehensive mapping of an application's object model.

When we are required to develop a GUI application for multiple styles, we should consider the following when developing its software architectural design:

- As discussed in Chapter 9, the user interface designer should be able to select the most efficient interaction components from a specific style guide. The software architecture of the GUI subsystems and its interfacing mechanisms must enable the invariant application functional core subsystem to be interfaced with the style-dependent GUI subsystem.
- Different style guides are associated with different computing platforms using a variety of user input devices (e.g., one-button mouse versus three-button mouse). The equivalent GUI components may respond to different user input events, or different sequences of user input events. The event responses will have to accommodate these differences.

11.8 TOOLKIT-INDEPENDENT SOFTWARE ARCHITECTURE

Style guides also have their respective reusable toolkit implementations to help develop style-complying applications. A user interface toolkit typically provides reusable GUI interaction components for the implementation of GUI subsystems, as well as interfacing mechanisms for the implementation of user interaction handling. Different toolkits usually have very different sets of interfacing mechanisms, software partitions, and programming-language binding.

Because of their ready availability, reusable toolkits are invaluable in any software development project. The challenge in developing a GUI application for multiple styles is accommodating the different interfacing mechanisms and software subsystems.

11.9 LOCALE-INDEPENDENT SOFTWARE ARCHITECTURE

Because of the language and cultural differences, locale independence requires extensive architectural design effort and additional software implementation effort for each locale to be supported.

The essential considerations in supporting different locales are the cultural differences, the type of characters, the scanning order, and the information translation. Each of these factors may result in very different GUI subsystem. To minimize implementation effort, a software architecture must further separate any of the locale-specific subsystems from the generic GUI subsystem.

11.10 SUMMARY

In this chapter, we have discussed the dialog-independent software architectures for GUI applications. The event-driven control flow with event-responses provides many advantages for a GUI application running on windowing environments.

We then examined the mapping of a user interface-level object model to software architectural design, along with the contextual GUI mapping.

In the next chapter, we look at various GUI environments and discuss the software tools for developing GUI on these environments.

CHAPTER 12

Implementing Graphical User Interface Software with Reusable Toolkits

*C*hapter 9 covered object-oriented GUI design by mapping object models into style-specific GUI interaction components. To implement such a design, we can choose from a number of reusable toolkits.

A reusable toolkit provides a foundation for both the software subsystems and the interface mechanisms of GUI applications. An object-oriented user interface toolkit, such as Motif, XView, and Open Look Intrinsic Toolkit (OLIT), provides the additional advantage of extendibility. An object-oriented application framework, such as MacApp and Borland ObjectWindows, provides basic application-functional-core classes in addition to its GUI classes.

Once we have selected a primary object-oriented toolkit to implement the GUI design, we must compose the user interface by instantiating the appropriate classes. The instance hierarchy, itself an aggregation object, is the realization of the GUI design, with all aspects of an object model being presented.

12.1 GRAPHICAL USER INTERFACE ENVIRONMENTS

GUI applications run on platforms with hardware and software support. The hardware support includes user input devices (e.g., mouse, keyboard) and graphics-display output devices (high-resolution graphics monitors). The software support includes the windowing-system software.

Windowing-system software manages the graphics resources of windows, mouse pointer, icons, colors, fonts, and graphics drawing primitives, to name several. It also handles the different types of events originated from user actions, window manager, and other application sources. Interapplication communication mechanisms are also provided to allow message passing among applications.

A graphical environment also provides layered abstraction of software libraries to assist the development of application software. These layers of abstraction allow application software to access various services provided by the graphical environment.

12.1.1 Graphics Resources and Their Management

A GUI application consumes extensive graphical resources including windows, mouse pointer, icons and bitmaps, colors, text strings and fonts, and drawing primitives. The performance of a GUI application relies on these services provided by the graphical environment.

Windows. Overlapping windows with various stacking orders allow the presentation of primary and secondary windows. In some window system toolkit implementations—for example, the style-specific toolkits (e.g., Motif, OLIT) based on the Xt Intrinsic layer for the X Window System— many of the GUI interaction components, or widgets, are implemented as windows.

Mouse Pointer. A mouse pointer provides visual feedback of current mouse-pointer position and the mode it is in. It is the key visual indicator for contextual feedback. A mouse pointer is a small bitmap image that defines its shape. The *hotspot* of a pointer indicates the mouse position.

Icons and Bitmaps. GUI applications use icons as one way to represent their source metaphors. An icon design based on a common source metaphor for a number of target locales would simplify the user interface development effort, because of the locale-independent nature of an icon representation.

Bitmaps are the fundamental data type for the pointer shapes, the icons, and images.

Colors. Graphics displays are capable of displaying monochrome, gray-scale, and color images. A bitmapped display device maintains a colormap to map the pixel values into actual display colors. The colormap and the display-video memory are limited resources shared by all applications running on the display.

Fonts and Text Strings. Even in GUI applications, textual information is still the major communication medium. However, with the numerous font types, styles, and sizes that are available, textual-information display becomes very flexible and appealing. The advances in scalable-font technology have also empowered graphical environments to support sophisticated desktop publishing applications.

Graphics Drawing Primitives. Graphics drawing primitives are the foundation of a graphical environment. The graphics primitives of lines and shapes are drawn on requests from applications. A GUI application uses many graphics drawing primitives to draw the user interface components of menus, push buttons, scrollbars, and so on. A GUI application with extensive output graphics (e.g., drawing and painting applications) also requires high-performance graphics drawing services.

12.1.2 Events of Different Sources

GUI applications adopt an event-responses interfacing mechanism to implement event-driven control flow. As the event occurs, it is sent to an event queue waiting for the application to respond. Event-driven control flow gives users a sense of control in their application sessions.

An event may come from different sources (see Figure 12-1). The graphical environments send user input events, and window-management events, such as resizing and visibility changes. A reusable toolkit may send events from additional sources—for example, file input/output events, interprocess communication read/write events, system interrupt events—to a GUI application.

Different graphical environments might use different terminology for the similar services. Table 12-1 lists a number of graphical environments and their event sources.

12.1.3 Interapplication Communication Mechanisms

In a graphical environment, a user may have more than one application running simultaneously, with each application performing specific functions. These applications may share data or rely on another application to provide specific information. In short, there may be relationships among the applications, just as there are relationships among the classes in an application's object model.

We can generalize the relationships among applications as relationships among objects in a larger object model, including all related applications. An individual application's object model becomes a subset of a larger object model encompassing many applications (see Figure 12-2).

Table 12–1 Events from User Input Devices, Window Management, and Other
Sources for Various Windowing Systems

	Apple Macintosh	Microsoft Windows	NextStep	X Window System
Keyboard	key-down key-up auto-key	WM_KEYDOWN WM_KEYUP	key-down key-up	KeyPress KeyRelease
Mouse	mouse-down mouse-up	WM_LBUTTONDBLCLK WM_LBUTTONDOWN WM_LBUTTONUP WM_MBUTTONDBLCLK WM_MBUTTONDOWN WM_MBUTTONUP WM_RBUTTONDBLCLK WM_RBUTTONDOWN WM_RBUTTONUP WM_MOUSEMOVE	mouse-down mouse-up mouse-moved mouse-dragged	ButtonPress ButtonRelease MotionNotify
Window Management	activate update	WM_SETFOCUS WM_KILLFOCUS WM_PAINT WM_ACTIVATE WM_ACTIVATEAPP WM_CANCELMODE WM_CHILDACTIVATE WM_CLOSE WM_CREATE WM_DESTROY WM_ENABLE WM_MOVE WM_QUIT WM_PARENTNOTIFY WM_SHOWWINDOW	mouse-entered mouse-exited window-exposed	FocusIn FocusOut EnterNotify LeaveNotify Expose GraphicsExpose NoExpose CirculateNotify ConfigureNotify CreateNotify DestroyNotify GravityNotify MapNotify MappingNotify ReparentNotify UnmapNotify VisibilityNotify
Interapplication Communication		WM_CUT WM_COPY WM_PASTE WM_DRAWCLIPBOARD WM_PAINTCLIPBOARD WM_DESTROYCLIPBOARD WM_DDE_INITIATE WM_DDE_TERMINATE WM_DDE_ADVISE WM_DDE_UNADVISE WM_DDE_REQUEST WM_DDE_ACK		ClientMessage PropertyNotify SelectionClear SelectionNotify SelectionRequest
Resource Change		WM_PALETTECHANGED WM_SYSCOLORCHANGE		ColormapNotify

As presented in Chapter 9, we can represent the relationships among the objects within a GUI application with different interaction models (e.g., pop-up dialog, drag-and-drop). Since, from a user interface software implementation

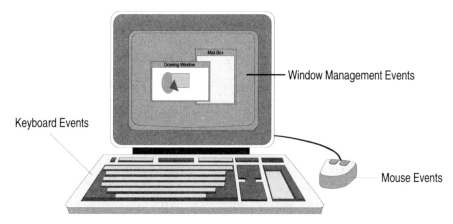

Figure 12–1. Events come from user input devices, window management, and other sources.

perspective, a dynamic relationship changes states of related objects, state changes must be reflected in the presentation of these objects. We can use function calls as the actual software mechanism to implement interobject communication within an application.

The graphical environment or the operating system provide interapplication communication mechanisms. We can find the following communication mechanisms in various graphical environments.

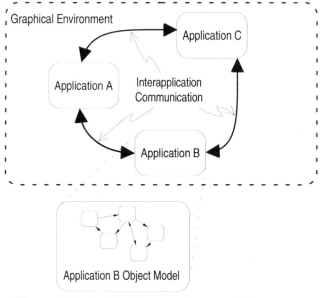

Figure 12–2. Applications running in a GUI environment.

1 **Cut-and-paste:** Many graphical environments provide the *clipboard* mechanism, in which the user first copies an object from an application into a clipboard, and later pastes it back into the same application or another application.

2 **Drag-and-drop:** Rather than presenting users with the indirect mechanism of *clipboard* metaphor, the drag-and-drop mechanism enables the user to copy, link, or move objects by direct manipulation.

3 **Object linking and embedding:** Object linking and embedding adopts a document-oriented model. In a document-oriented model, a compound document (an aggregation class) created by a client application may contain various data objects linked to different server applications (component classes that can be part of an aggregation class). With object linking mechanism, a client document is automatically updated if there is any change in the server data object.

The order of these individual mechanisms has an increasing level of sophistication. Although each of these mechanisms requires a varying degree of implementation effort, they all allow direct control by a user. After all, users are the best judge on how objects from various applications should be linked to perform specific tasks.

In different GUI environments, we can find various interapplication communication mechanisms being supported. Table 12-2 lists the interapplication communication mechanisms for a number of GUI environments. These mechanisms provide user-level access, rather than the application programmer-level access. Dynamic data exchange (DDE) in Microsoft Windows environment, Apple Event in Macintosh System 7, and interprocess communication (IPC) and remote procedure calls (RPC) in UNIX operating system are examples of low-level interapplication communication mechanisms not considered here.

Table **12–2** Interapplication Communication Mechanisms Supported by Various GUI Environments

Apple Macintosh System 7	IBM OS/2 2.0	Microsoft Windows 3.1	OSF/Motif 1.2	OPEN LOOK
Cut-and-Paste	Cut-and-Paste	Cut-and-Paste	Cut-and-Paste	Cut-and-Paste
	Drag-and-Drop	Drag-and-Drop	Drag-and-Drop	Drag-and-Drop
Publish and Subscribe		Object Linking and Embedding		

12.2 USER INTERFACE SOFTWARE DEVELOPMENT ENVIRONMENT

Many of the services provided by a graphical environment are implemented in different levels of abstraction. The requirements of portability, and customizability would favor intermediate layers between primitive system-level services and the application software.

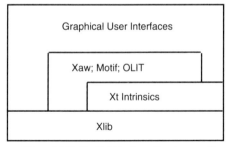 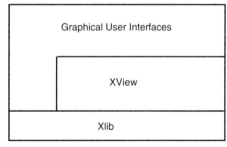

Figure 12–3. X Window System software development environment.

Reusable toolkits are layered in a number of ways. In the X Window System, a number of style-specific toolkits are available with different layering architecture (see Figure 12-3). Other graphical environments also provide their own layered toolkit libraries. Within each layer, there are finer partitions of specific services. We examine the software architecture of a number of graphical environments in the following sections.

12.2.1 Apple Macintosh Software Development

The Apple Macintosh graphical environment (Apple 1991) established many of the industry's first de facto standards. Its comprehensive *User Interface Toolbox* provides various resource services to support a GUI application. The services fall into the following categories (see Figure 12-4):

- **Graphics Resources:** The QuickDraw component supports all display drawing operations in a Macintosh. The Color Manager and the Palette Manager provide color-resource services. The Font Manager provides text-rendering services.

- **GUI Interaction Components:** The Dialog Manager handles dialog and alert boxes (error, warning messages). The Menu Manager handles menu bar and pulldown menus. The Control Manager provides control components like buttons, check boxes, and scrollbars. The List Manager supports one-dimensional and two-dimensional lists. The TextEdit component offers text-editing services.

- **Graphical Environment Services:** The Event Manager dispatches events of various sources to an application. The Window Manager manages the creation, moving, resizing, and closing of windows on a display. The scrap manager provides the clipboard for transferring data between application programs.

The *MacApp* layer (Wilson, Rosenstein, and Shafer 1990) is an object-oriented application framework introduced in the mid-1980s. The MacApp layer

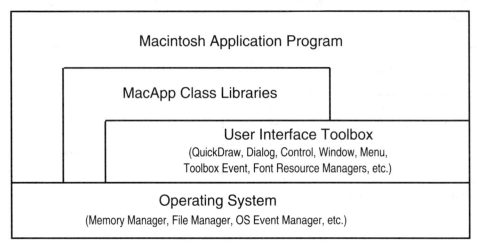

Figure 12–4. Macintosh software development environment.

includes classes that provide high-level services of data structures, system resources, and user interface services. We describe the MacApp class hierarchy further in Section 12.3.1.

12.2.2 Microsoft Windows 3.x Application Development

There are a number of toolkits that support the development of GUI applications to run on the Microsoft Windows 3.x graphical environment. Depending on the software vendor of the development tools, the levels of software abstraction may be different in each separate layer, and the class hierarchy can be quite different (see Figure 12-5).

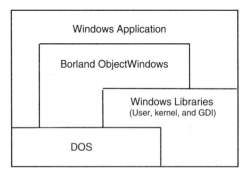 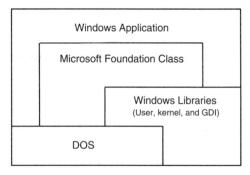

Figure 12–5. Microsoft Windows 3.x software development environment.

The software layer of the Windows libraries has three main components:

- **User library:** The user library provides window-management services for all application windows running in the Windows environment. It also provides the user interface components of menus, dialog boxes, list boxes, scrollbars, and so on; handles user inputs from keyboard and mouse input devices; and provides the clipboard services for interapplication communication.

* **Kernel library:** The kernel library provides the functions of resource management, memory management, task scheduling, and DOS interfacing.
* **Graphics Device Interface (GDI) library:** The GDI library provides drawing primitives for the graphics display and printer devices. The line-drawing, font- and text-drawing, and the color-palette modules are examples of GDI library functions.

In Figure 12-5, we have also shown the software layering using the Borland ObjectWindows and Microsoft Foundation Class application frameworks to develop applications for the Windows environment. In the next section, we will look further into the Borland ObjectWindows class hierarchy.

12.2.3 NextStep Application Development

The NextStep environment (NeXT 1991) is made up of several components as shown in Figure 12-6. For application development, a developer would use the Application Kit and the Interface Builder extensively.

The Application Kit is an application framework that includes a large number of classes. The services provided by the Application Kit classes include basic user interface components, event-driven control-flow mechanisms, data structures, and many other system utilities. In Section 12.3.3, we will look further into the Application Kit class hierarchy.

The NextStep Interface Builder is a rapid-prototyping tool that greatly reduces the implementation effort of a GUI application in many ways. Because its underlying software layer (the Application Kit) is an application framework, the NextStep Interface Builder provides functions beyond a typical user interface rapid-prototyping tool. A good portion of a NextStep application functional core subsystem may be developed by using the NextStep Interface Builder.

12.2.4 Xt Intrinsics-Based Software Development

The Xt Intrinsics software layer implements a number of mechanisms for object-oriented programming, geometry management, resource management, and event management in C language (Asente and Swick 1990).

Object-Oriented Programming Mechanism. The Xt Intrinsics object-oriented programming mechanisms include (single) inheritance, base classes, and data hiding. Although these mechanisms are at times cumbersome to use when compared with using an object-oriented programming language such as C++, they have provided invaluable services to ease the transition of C language programmers into object-oriented programming practices.

Integral to this object-oriented mechanism is a collection of base classes

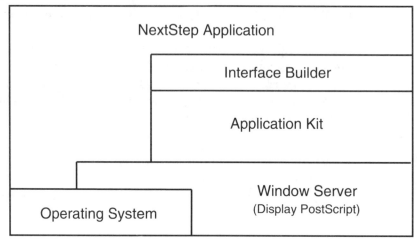

Figure 12–6. The NextStep software development environment.

that establish the foundation of many Xt-based widget hierarchies, such as the Athena widget set (Xaw), the Motif widget set, and the OPEN LOOK Intrinsics Toolkit (OLIT).

Geometry Management. Because of various geometry requirements and conflicts among the children instances of a composite widget, as well as between the parent and a child in a user interface layout, the geometry-management mechanism is provided to resolve these problems. The composite widget classes also have a geometry-manager method to manage the size, position, and stacking order of their children.

Resource Management. Each of the Xt Intrinsics-based widget classes maintains a record of data that defines the state of each widget instance. This record of state information is called resources. The Xt Intrinsics layer also provides mechanisms to allow resource value specification of various widget instances in the instance hierarchy. The dynamic behavior of a GUI application is implemented with **XtSetValues** function call, which changes the resource values of widget instances.

Event Management. The Xt Intrinsics layer provides mechanisms to handle events originated from the X window server and other sources. An application registers event handlers, action translations, and callbacks as response functions. As an event occurs, it is dispatched to the corresponding response function of a specific window.

12.2.5 OSF/Motif Application Development

The OSF/Motif widget set is implemented as a software layer above the Xt Intrinsics toolkit (see Figure 12-7). A Motif GUI application is composed of Motif widget instances. By setting the resource values of widget instances, the dynamic behavior of the GUI is realized. We will examine the Motif widget class hierarchy further in a later section.

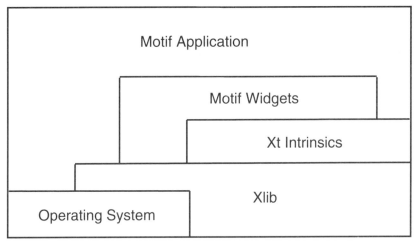

Figure 12–7. The Motif software development environment.

12.2.6 OPEN LOOK Application Development with OLIT

Similar to the Motif application development, an OPEN LOOK GUI is composed of the OLIT widget instances, while the dynamic behavior is implemented by setting the resource values of these widget instances (see Figure 12-8). We discuss the OLIT widget class hierarchy later in this chapter.

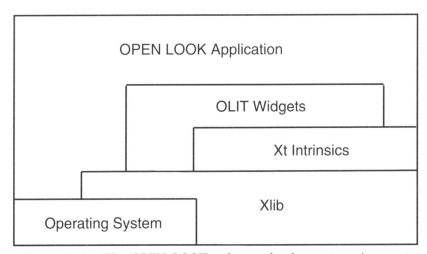

Figure 12–8. The OPEN LOOK software development environment using OLIT.

12.2.7 OPEN LOOK Application Development with XView Toolkit

The XView toolkit is another implementation of OPEN LOOK style. The application programmer's interface was developed to ease transition of SunView applications onto the X Window System environment. Different from Xt Intrinsics based toolkits, XView implements its own mechanisms to emulate object-orientation in C language. From the software developer's perspective, the XView toolkit sits directly above the Xlib layer, without an Xt Intrinsics-like intermediate layer (see Figure 12-9).

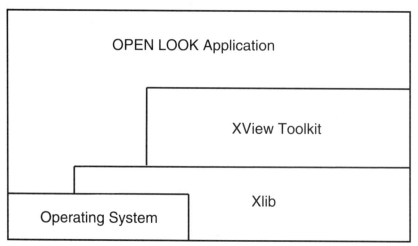

Figure 12–9.   The OPEN LOOK software development environment with XView toolkit.

12.3 OBJECT-ORIENTED GRAPHICAL USER INTERFACE TOOLKITS

In the last section, we discussed the software layer frequently used in application development—the object-oriented toolkit layer. Depending on the intended purpose of these object-oriented toolkits, there are two types of GUI toolkits. One type offers a number of classes implementing GUI interaction components; the other provides an application framework.

- **Interaction-components toolkit:** Interaction objects are the user interface components of windows, menus, scrollbars, and other control elements. The interaction objects of a toolkit usually conform to a certain user interface style guide. To develop a style-specific GUI, the interaction objects are selected to compose the presentation aspect of it. The implementation of these classes would also allow the application functional core subsystem to be connected with the user interface. The Motif and OLIT widget sets and the XView toolkit are examples of object-oriented toolkits offering interaction objects.

- **Application-framework toolkit:** In addition to the interaction objects found in other user interface toolkits, an application framework provides several classes for the development of other partitions (i.e., models and controllers) of an application. In an application framework, there are often the additional classes to provide event-driven control flow mechanisms and common data structures (e.g., arrays, lists, trees, hash tables). The MacApp, NextStep Application Kit, Microsoft Foundation Class Library, and Borland C++/ObjectWindows are examples of application frameworks.

In the next subsections, we present the classes hierarchy of a number of object-oriented toolkits. Despite the different GUI environments, there are some similarities among them.

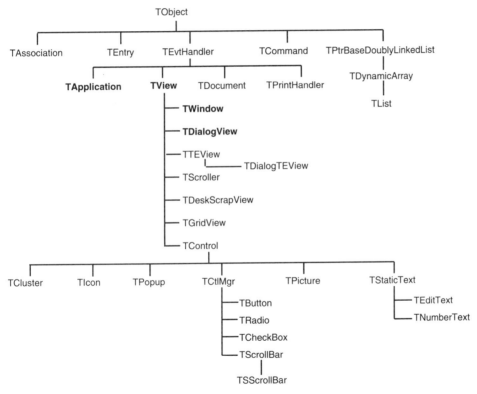

Figure 12–10. MacApp application-framework class hierarchy.

12.3.1 MacApp Classes

The MacApp class hierarchy (shown in Figure 12-10) consists of the root class of TObject and many other subclasses to provide an application framework. As an application framework, the MacApp class libraries offer services beyond those of a user interface toolkit (Wilson, Rosenstein, and Shafer 1990). For example, the event-driven control-flow mechanism class (TApplication), the data-structure classes (TDynamicArray, TPtrBasedDoublyLinkedList), the user-action and state tracking class (TCommand—also supports undo and redo commands), and system-utility classes (TPrintHandler) offer functions beyond the user interface presentation and behavior services to include a number of general services for the application functional core subsystem of an application.

To compose the presentation of a Macintosh user interface application, the MacApp classes of TWindow, TView, and their subclasses are used extensively. Each of an application's top-level primary and secondary windows is an instance of the TWindow class. Each instance of a TWindow class is associated with one instance of a TView class, which in turn contains an instance hierarchy of view objects. The TView class and many of its subclasses are *composite* classes, which can contain children instances of other composite classes or primitive classes.

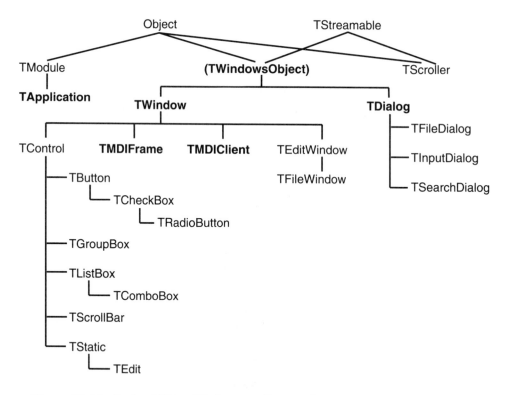

Figure 12–11. Borland ObjectWindows application-framework class hierarchy.

12.3.2 Borland ObjectWindows Classes

The Borland ObjectWindows class library (Borland 1991) provides interaction classes for the development of a GUI application running in the Microsoft Windows environment (see Figure 12-11). The Borland ObjectWindows class library is used with the Borland C++ integrated development environment, which uses many sophisticated object-oriented programming features provided by the C++ language. For example, the extensive use of templates for the container class library implementation produces very compact and efficient code. The integrated development environment, along with a large number of data structures and user interface classes, qualify it as a GUI application-framework environment.

The ObjectWindows class library is part of an application framework that includes other class libraries (e.g., the container class library). The TApplication class provides the event-driven control-flow mechanism. Many of the subclasses of the TWindowObject abstract class are composite classes that can contain children window instances. Instances of the TWindow class implement the top-level windows of a GUI application's primary windows. Instances of the TDialog class implements the top-level windows of the secondary windows. There is also the TControl class with subclasses of GUI control components.

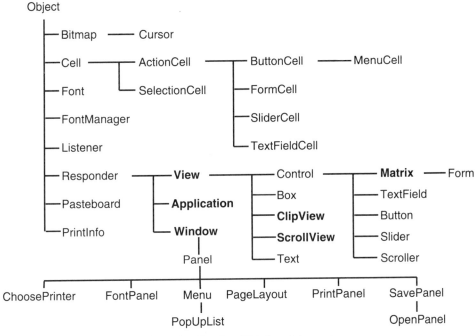

Figure 12–12. The NextStep Application-Kit class hierarchy.

12.3.3 NextStep Application Kit

The NextStep Application Kit is an application framework (NeXT 1991). The Application Kit inheritance hierarchy contains a large number of classes to provide event-driven control flow, GUI components, and common dialogs (see Figure 12-12).

The Application class provides a framework for every application to run by maintaining a list of all the Window objects and by dispatching events to the

Responder objects in the application. Instances of the Window class are the top-level windows of the an application's primary windows. Instances of the Panel class are the top-level windows of an application's secondary windows. The Menu objects are the top-level window for the menus. Each instance of the Window and the Panel class is associated with a View object, which in turn contains a view hierarchy with superview and subviews to construct a NextStep GUI. The Menu objects are also organized in a hierarchy of supermenu and submenus. The Speaker and Listener classes implement the interapplication communication mechanism.

12.3.4 Xt Intrinsics-Based Toolkits

The Xt Intrinsics software layer provides a number of base classes to establish the object-oriented programming mechanisms without any specific look-and-feel policy (see Figure 12-13). These base classes form the foundation of the Motif widget set and the OLIT widget set to be examined in this section.

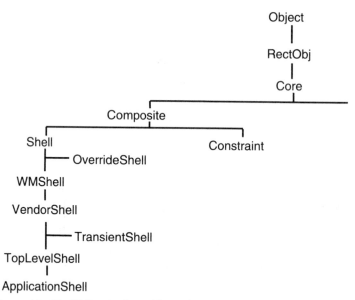

Figure 12–13. Xt Intrinsics widget class hierarchy.

Most notable of these base classes are the two subclasses of the Core widget class, namely the Primitive widget class (found in respective widget-set inheritance hierarchy) and the Composite widget class. Subclasses of the composite widget class are containers that can contain children, which can be instances of the Composite widget classes and the Primitive widget classes.

Subclasses of the Primitive widget class implement basic GUI control components such as push buttons, and scrollbars. Instances of the Primitive widget classes cannot contain children. Instances of the Shell widget classes serve as the top-level windows of an application to communicate with the window manager. The Constraint class is an abstract class; its subclasses may implement complex geometry-management functions to manage the position, size, and stacking order of their children windows on behalf of children's geometry-constraint specification.

Motif Toolkit. The Motif toolkit (Young 1991, Open Software Foundation 1991b) is a set of widget classes implemented as subclasses of Xt Intrinsics-based widget classes (see Figure 12-14). The XmManager, XmPrimitive, and XmGadget are the Motif classes serving as the abstract base classes to their subclasses. These Motif base classes implement the basic Motif user interface style, such as the three-dimensional look and the tab group traversal navigation.

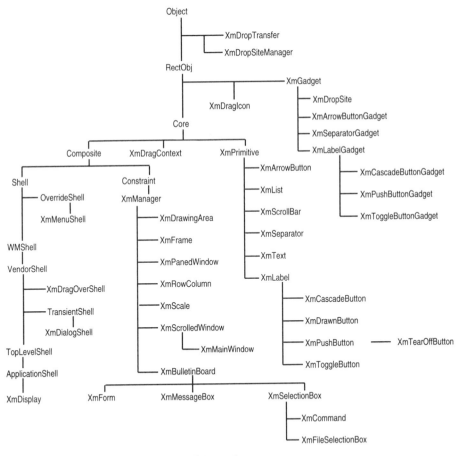

Figure 12–14. Motif widget class hierarchy.

Motif toolkit provides two additional Shell widget classes. The XmDialogShell widget class is derived from the TransientShell widget class to serve as the top-level window of a pop-up dialog. The XmMenuShell widget class is derived from the OverrideShell widget class to serve as the top-level window of a menu.

The subclasses of the XmManager class provide geometry-management functions to manage their children. The XmPanedWindow and the XmForm widget classes offer functions of the Constraint widget class that accommodate the layout-geometry constraints specified by their children.

The XmGadget class is derived from the Xt Intrinsics RectObj class. Instances of the XmGadget and its subclasses are windowless. They must have a Motif XmManager widget class (or its subclasses) instance as the parent window to handle window events and requests on their behalf, and they cannot contain children. The subclasses of XmGadget provide the windowless implementation of basic GUI elements.

OPEN LOOK Intrinsics Toolkit (OLIT). OLIT (Young and Pew 1992) is an Xt Intrinsics-based widget set that implements the OPEN LOOK user interface style (see Figure 12-15). The OLIT widget set provides the EventObj, Manager, and Primitive classes as the base classes, providing basic OPEN LOOK user interface style implementation.

The OLIT widget set provides the additional Shell widget classes of MenuShell, NoticeShell, and PopupWindowShell that are derived from the Xt Intrinsics TransientShell widget class. While the Motif widget-set implementation derives the XmMenuShell class from the Xt Intrinsics OverrideShell class, the MenuShell class of OLIT is a subclass of the TransientShell class. An instance of the MenuShell class communicates with the OPEN LOOK window manager to specify the characteristics such as the window title, the pushpin state, and other window-manager hints. To implement multiple primary windows for an application, instances of the BaseWindowShell class are used.

Similar to the Motif widget implementation, the OLIT widget set has the RubberTile and the Form widget class that implement complex geometry-management functions to allow their children to specify preferred layout-geometry constraints.

In addition to offering the Gadget classes (MenuButtonGadget and Oblong-ButtonGadget) that consume less computing resources, the OLIT widget set also offers Flat widget classes that contain children of a given class. The Flat widget classes require much less memory space. In the most recent release of OLIT (release 3.0), there are three Flat widget classes, namely the FlatExclusives, FlatNonexclusives, and FlatCheckBox, which contain RectButton or CheckBox children.

12.3.5 XView Toolkit

The XView toolkit (Heller 1991) implements OPEN LOOK user interface

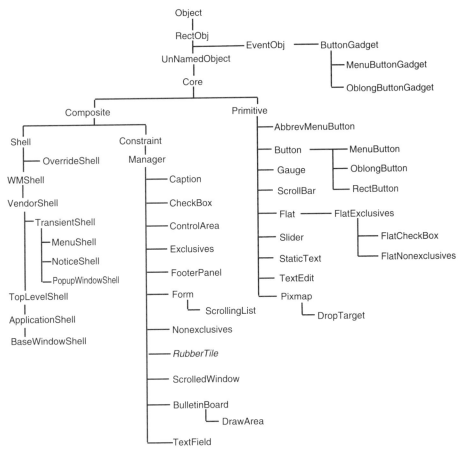

Figure 12–15. OLIT widget class hierarchy.

style interaction components. Although XView also provides mechanisms to support object-oriented programming, the architecture of the XView toolkit is quite different from Xt Intrinsics-based toolkits. For example, the class hierarchy does not have the clear branching of Composite and Primitive classes as in Xt Intrinsics-based toolkits (see Figure 12-16). The classes in the XView inheritance hierarchy are called packages.

An instance of the Frame package functions as both a top-level window and a composite containing children. The Panel package may contain a number of children to implement the OPEN LOOK control area. The Canvas package is used to implement an application's work space. It can also have children.

12.4 USER INTERFACE RAPID-PROTOTYPING TOOLS

Depending on the extent of functions provided and the supporting mechanisms used, there are several categories of user interface prototyping tools. Cur-

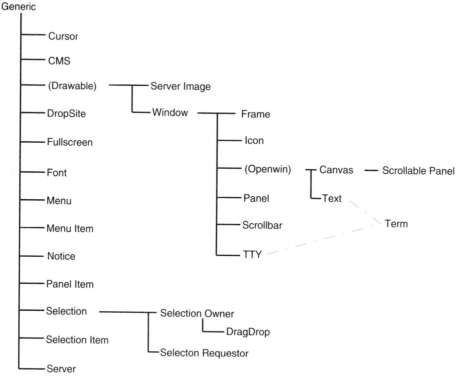

Figure 12–16. XView class hierarchy.

rently, the commercially available GUI rapid-prototyping tools are largely limited to prototyping the static aspects of user interface presentation layer. The two most common categories are:

1 **User interface management system (UIMS):** provides a development tool for specifying the presentation and the behavior of a user interface and, sometimes, a run-time counterpart is required to manage the dynamic behavior of a GUI (Hix 1990).

2 **Interactive design tool (IDT):** allows a user to compose the presentation component of a GUI by direct manipulation.

We can find a number of rapid-prototyping tools in many of the popular GUI environments. The few commercial products mentioned here are a small sample from a large number of available selections in each of the graphical environments we have examined in this chapter.

- MacApp application developers use the ViewEdit tool to compose the user interface presentation instance hierarchy of various view objects. They use the ResEdit tool to create the graphics resources of menus, dialogs, cursors, icons, and bitmaps.

- For Windows 3.x application development, the Borland C++ provides the Resource Workshop for the composition of menus, dialogs, cursors, icons, and bitmaps.
- For Motif application development, there are a number of rapid-prototyping tools offered by software vendors or system vendors (e.g., the Interface Architect offered by Hewlett-Packard for its HP-UX workstations and the AIX Interface Composer (AIC) offered by IBM for its RS/6000 workstations.
- The sophiscated Interface Builder is an integral component of the NextStep environment that allows a developer to prototype both the presentation and the behavior of a user interface.
- For OPEN LOOK application development, the interactive development tool of devGuide is offered by SunSoft for the composition of user interface presentation adhering to the OPEN LOOK style.

12.5 SUMMARY

In this chapter, we have examined various GUI environments, GUI software development environments, object-oriented toolkits and application frameworks, and GUI rapid-prototyping tools. The selection of some combination of these environments and development tools is dictated by the requirements specification. For any specific GUI environment, the choices of development tools are limited and still insufficient in several respects.

The object-oriented life-cycle approach in this book should help developers control the complexity of their GUI applications by focusing on the high-level abstraction of the application, namely the application's object model. Regardless of any constraints placed by the requirements specification, the object model and the task model are the two fundamental representations of an application.

Bibliography

Anderson, John R. (1989) "A Theory of the Origins of Human Knowledge." *Artificial Intelligence* 40, September, pp. 313-51.

Anderson, John R. (1990) *Cognitive Psychology and Its Implications.* New York: W.H. Freeman & Company.

Apple Computer. (1987) *Human Interface Guidelines: The Apple Desktop Interface.* Reading, Mass.: Addison-Wesley.

Apple Computer. (1991) *Inside Macintosh Volume VI.* Reading, Mass.: Addison-Wesley.

Arnold, Patrick, Stephanie Bodoff, Derek Coleman, Helena Gilchrist, and Fiona Hayes. (1991) "An Evaluation of Five Object-Oriented Development Methods." HP Laboratories Technical Report HPL-91-41.

Asente, Paul, and Ralph Swick. (1990) *The X Window System Toolkit.* Bedford, Mass.: Digital Press.

Barth, Paul S. (1986) "An Object-Oriented Approach to Graphical Interfaces." *ACM Trans. on Graphics* 5, no. 2, pp. 142-72.

Booch, Grady. (1991) *Object-Oriented Design: with Applications.* Redwood City, Calif.: Benjamin / Cummings.

Borland. (1991) *ObjectWindows for C++: User's Guide.* Scotts Valley, Calif.: Borland.

Bovair, Susan, David E. Kieras, and Peter G. Polson. (1990) "The Acquisition and Performance of Text-Editing Skill: A Cognitive Complexity Analysis." *Human Computer Interaction* 5, pp. 1-48.

Card, Stuart K., Thomas P. Moran, and Allen Newell. (1983) *The Psychology of Human-Computer Interaction*. Hillsdale, N.J.: Lawrence Erlbaum Associates.

Cardelli, Luca, and Peter Wegner. (1985) "On Understanding Types, Data Abstraction, and Polymorphism." *ACM Computing Surveys* 17, no. 4, December, pp. 471-522.

Carroll, John M., and Judith Reitman Olson, (1988) "Mental Models in Human-Computer Interaction." *Handbook of Human-Computer Interaction* (Martin Helander, ed.), Amsterdam: North-Holland, Ch. 2, pp. 45-65.

Carroll, John M., Robert L. Mack, and Wendy A. Kellog. (1988) "Interface Metaphors and User Interface Design." *Handbook of Human-Computer Interaction* (Martin Helander, ed.), Amsterdam: North-Holland, Ch. 3, pp. 67-85.

Casner, Stephen M. (1991) "A Task-Analytic Approach to the Automated Design of Graphic Presentation." *ACM Trans. Graphics* 10, no. 2, April, pp. 111-51.

de Champeaux, Dennis. (1991) "A Comparative Study of Object-Oriented Analysis Methods." HP Laboratories Technical Report HPL-91-41, April.

Chen, Peter. (1976) "The Entity-Relationship Model—Toward A Unified View of Data." *ACM Trans. Database Systems* 1, no. 1, March, pp. 9-36.

Clement, Catherine A., and Dedre Gentner. (1991) "Systematicity as a Selection Constraint in Analogical Mapping." *Cognitive Science* 15, pp. 89-132.

Coad, Peter, and Edward Yourdon. (1991) *Object-Oriented Analysis*. Englewood Cliffs, N.J.: Yourdon Press.

Connell, John L., and Linda Brice Shafer. (1989) *Structured Rapid Prototyping: An Evolutionary Approach to Software Development*. Englewood Cliffs, N.J.: Prentice-Hall.

Cox, Brad J. (1986) *Object-Oriented Programming: An Evolutionary Approach*. Reading, Mass.: Addison-Wesley.

Danforth, Scott, and Chris Tomlinson. (1988) "Type Theories and Object-Oriented Programming." *ACM Computing Surveys* 20, no. 1, March, pp. 29-72.

Davis, Alan M. (1990) *Software Requirements: Analysis and Specification*. Englewood Cliffs, N.J.: Prentice-Hall.

Egan, Dennis E. (1988) "Individual Differences in Human-Computer Interaction." *Handbook of Human-Computer Interaction* (Martin Helander, ed.), Amsterdam: North-Holland, Ch. 24, pp. 543-68.

Elkerton, Jay. (1988) "Online Aiding for Human-Computer Interfaces." *Handbook of Human-Computer Interaction* (Martin Helander, ed.), Amsterdam: North-Holland, Ch. 16, pp. 345-64.

Falkenhainer, Brian, Kenneth D. Forbus, and Dedre Gentner. (1989) "The Structure-Mapping Engine: Algorithm and Examples." *Artificial Intelligence* 41, no. 2, pp. 1-63.

Foley, James D., Andries van Dam, Steven K. Feiner, and John G. Hughes. (1990) *Computer Graphics: Principles and Practice*. Reading, Mass.: Addison-Wesley.

Gentner, Dedre. (1983) "Structure-Mapping: A Theoretical Framework for Analogy." *Cognitive Science* 7, pp. 155-70.

Goldberg, Adele. (1984) *Smalltalk-80: The Interactive Programming Environment*. Reading, Mass.: Addison-Wesley.

Gong, Richard, and Jay Elkerton. (1990) "Designing Minimal Documentation Using GOMS Model: A Usability Evaluation of an Engineering Approach." *CHI'90 Conference Proceedings*, 1990, pp. 99-106.

Hall, Rogers P. (1989) "Computational Approaches to Analogical Reasoning: A Comparative Analysis." *Artificial Intelligence* 39, no. 1, pp. 39-120.

Hartson, H. Rex, and Deborah Hix. (1989) "Human-Computer Interface Development: Concepts and Systems for Its Management." *ACM Computing Surveys* 21, no. 1, March, pp. 5-92.

Heller, Dan. (1991) *XView Programming Manual*. Sebastopol, Calif.: O'Reilly & Associates, Inc.

Hix, Deborah. (1990) "Generations of User-Interface Management Systems." *IEEE Software,* September 1990, pp. 77-87.

Holyoak, Keith J., and Paul Thagard. (1989) "Analogical Mapping by Constraint Satisfaction." *Cognitive Science* 13, pp. 295-355.

Hull, Richard, and Roger King. (1987) "Semantic Database Modeling: Survey, Applications, and Research Issues." *ACM Computing Surveys* 19, no. 3, September, pp. 201-60.

IBM. (1989) *System Application Architecture: Common User Access Advanced Interface Design Guide.* SC26-4582-0, IBM, June.

IBM. (1991a) *System Application Architecture: Common User Access Guide to User Interface Design.* SC34-4289-00, IBM, October.

IBM. (1991b) *System Application Architecture: Common User Access Advanced Interface Design Reference.* SC34-4290-00, IBM, October.

John, Bonnie E. (1988) "Contributions to Engineering Models of Human-Computer Interaction." Ph.D. dissertation, Department of Psychology, Carnegie Mellon University.

John, Bonnie E. (1990) "Extension of GOMS Analyses to Expert Performance Requiring Perception of Dynamic Visual and Auditory Information." *CHI'90 Conference Proceedings*, pp. 107-15.

John, Bonnie E., Alonso H. Vera, and Allen Newell. (1990) "Towards Real-Time GOMS." School of Computer Science, Carnegie Mellon University, Technical Report CMU-CS-90-195.

Johnson, Mark. (1987) *The Body in the Mind.* Chicago: University of Chicago Press.

Kieras, David E. (1988) "Towards a Practical GOMS Model Methodology for User Interface Design." *Handbook of Human-Computer Interaction* (Martin Helander, ed.), Amsterdam: North-Holand, Ch. 7, pp. 345-62.

Kieras, David E. (1991) "A Guide to GOMS Task Analysis." CHI'91 Tutorial note, Winter.

Kim, Won. (1990) "Object-Oriented Databases: Definition and Research Directions." *IEEE Trans. Knowledge and Data Engineering* 2, no. 3, September, pp. 327-41.

Krasner, Glenn E., and Stephen T. Pope. (1988) "A Cookbook for Using the Model-View-Controller User Interface Paradigm in Smalltalk-80." *Journal of Object-Oriented Programming* 1, no. 3, August/September, pp. 26-49.

Lakoff, George, and Mark Johnson. (1980) *Metaphors We Live By.* Chicago: University of Chicago Press.

Lakoff, George. (1987) *Women, Fire, and Dangerous Things: What Categories Reveal about the Mind.* Chicago: University of Chicago Press.

Laurel, Brenda, editor. (1990) *The Art of Human-Computer Interface Design.* Reading, Mass.: Addison-Wesley.

Linton, Mark A., John M. Vlissides, and Paul R. Calder. (1989) "Composing User Interfaces with InterViews, *IEEE Computer* 22, no. 2, Feb., pp. 8-22.

Liu, Ling. (1992) "Exploring Semantics in Aggregation Hierarchies for Object-Oriented Databases." *IEEE Proceedings of the 8th International Conference on Data Engineering,* pp. 116-25.

Marcus, Aaron. (1992) *Graphic Design for Electronic Documents and User Interface.* Reading, Mass.: Addison-Wesley.

Mayer, Richard E. (1988) "From Novice to Expert." in *Handbook of Human-Computer Interaction* (Martin Helander, ed.), Amsterdam: North-Holland, Ch. 25, pp. 569-80.

Meyer, Bertrand. (1988) *Object-Oriented Software Construction.* Englewood Cliffs, N.J.: Prentice-Hall.

Microsoft. (1992) *The Windows Interface: An Application Design Guide.* Microsoft Windows Version 3.1, Microsoft.

Minsky, Marvin. (1975) "A Framework for Representing Knowledge." *The Psychology of Computer Vision* (P. Winston, ed.), New York: McGraw-Hill.

Myers, Brad A. (1991) "Separating Application Code from Toolkits: Eliminating the Spaghetti of Callbacks." Proceedings *ACM Symposium on User Interface Software and Technology,* pp. 211-20.

NeXT. (1991) *NextStep Environment:* Concepts. NeXT, Inc.

Norman, Donald A. (1988) *The Design of Everyday Things.* New York: Doubleday.

Open Software Foundation. (1991a) *OSF/Motif: Style Guide.* Englewood Cliffs, N.J.: Prentice-Hall.

Open Software Foundation. (1991b) *OSF/Motif: Programmer's Guide.* Englewood Cliffs, N.J.: Prentice-Hall.

Raap, Kenneth R., and Renate J. Roske-Hofstrand. (1988) "Design of Menus." *Handbook of Human-*

Computer Interaction (Martin Helander, ed.), Amsterdam: North-Holland, Ch. 10, pp. 205-35.

Rumbaugh, James, Michael Blaha, William Premerlani, Frederick Eddy, and William Lorensen (1991) *Object-Oriented Modeling and Design*, Englewood Cliffs, N.J.: Prentice-Hall.

Shan, Yen-Ping. (1990) "MoDE: A UIMS for Smalltalk." *ECCOP/OOPSLA '90 Proceedings*, October, pp. 258-68.

Shlaer, Sally, and Stephen J. Mellor. (1988) *Object-Oriented Systems Analysis: Modeling the World in Data*. Englewood Cliffs, N.J.: Yourdon Press.

Shlaer, Sally, and Stephen J. Mellor. (1992) *Object Life Cycles: Modeling the World in States*. Englewood Cliffs, N.J.: Yourdon Press.

Shneiderman, Ben. (1992) *Designing the User Interface: Strategies for Effective Human-Computer Interaction*. Reading, Mass.: Addison-Wesley.

Smith, John Miles, and Diane C.P. Smith. (1977) "Database Abstractions: Aggregation and Generalization." *ACM Trans. Database Systems* 2, no. 2, June, pp. 105-33.

Stefik, Mark, and Daniel G. Bobrow. (1986) "Object-Oriented Programming: Themes and Variations." *AI Magazine* 6, no. 4, Winter, pp. 40-62.

Stroustrup, Bjarne. (1988) "What Is Object-Oriented Programming?" *IEEE Software*, May, pp. 10-20.

Sun Microsystems. (1990) *OPEN LOOK; Graphical User Interface Application Style Guidelines*. Reading, Mass.: Addison-Wesley.

Teorey, Toby J., DongQing Yang, and James P. Fry. (1986) "A Logical Design Methodology for Relational Databases Using the Extended Entity-Relationship Model." *ACM Computing Surveys* 18, no. 2, June, pp. 197-220.

Thimbleby, Harold. (1990) *User Interface Design*. New York: ACM Press.

Wang, Haiying, and Mark Green. (1991) "An Event-Object Recovery Model for Object-Oriented User Interfaces." *Proceedings ACM Symposium on User Interface Software and Technology*, pp. 107-15.

Ward, Paul T. "How to Integrate Object Orientation with Structured Analysis and Design." *IEEE Software*, March 1989, pp. 74-82.

Wilson, David A., Larry S. Rosenstein, and Dan Shafer. (1990) *C++ Programming with MacApp*. Reading, Mass.: Addison-Wesley.

Wirfs-Brock, Rebecca, Brian Wilkerson, and Lauren Wiener. (1990) *Designing Object-Oriented Software*. Englewood Cliffs, N.J.: Prentice-Hall.

Young, Douglas A. (1990) *The X Window System Programming and Applications with Xt: OSF/Motif Edition*. Englewood Cliffs, N.J.: Prentice-Hall.

Young, Douglas A., and John A. Pew. (1992) *The X Window System Programming and Applications with Xt: OPEN LOOK Edition*. Englewood Cliffs, N.J.: Prentice-Hall.

Yourdon, Edward. (1989) *Modern Structured Analysis*. Englewood Cliffs, N. J.: Yourdon Press.

Index

AUTOBAHN SYSTEMS, INC.

41027 Canyon Heights Drive, Fremont, CA 94539-3880 USA Phone (510)438-0386 FAX (510)438-0387

Products and Services

Autobahn Systems, Inc., offers software development tools, training courses, and professional services in object-oriented GUI application development.

Software Development Tools

- GUI App: Design™: Available for Windows 3.0 and above. Following the approach presented in this book, this GUI application is for object modeling and system-level design of user interface applications.

Training Courses

- Object-Oriented GUI Application Development: This course uses the approach presented in this book, including analysis, design, and implementation activities.
- Customized Training Courses: Our courses can be tailored to your specific needs in user interface styles and software requirements.

Professional Services

- Consulting and Software Engineering Services: Autobahn Systems, Inc., provides consulting and software engineering services in client/server software development.

For software purchase and more information about these products and services, detach and mail (or fax) this reply card or call (510)438-0386.

❑ Please send me _____ copies of *GUI App: Design*™ for Windows at $59* each. $_____
Sales tax (CA customers add 8.25%) $_____
Freight ($5 by UPS in United States lower 48 states) $_____
Total $_____

Check the appropriate disk option: ❑ 3.5" high-density   ❑ 5.25" high-density

*LIMITED TIME OFFER THROUGH 10/31/93. Payment in U.S. funds. Do not send cash or purchase order. Make checks payable to Autobahn Systems, Inc. Your check will be deposited immediately upon receipt. Your credit card will be charged upon shipment.

Payment Method: ❑ check or money order enclosed   ❑VISA   ❑Mastercard
Card Number_|__|__|__|__|__|__|__|__|__|__|__|__|__|__|__| Expiration Date_____

Cardholder's Signature_____

Please send me more information about:
❑ Software Development Tools   ❑ Training Courses   ❑ Professional Services

Name_____ Title_____

Company_____ Department/Mail Stop_____

Address_____

City_____ State/Province_____

Zip/Postal Code_____ Country_____

Phone_____ Fax_____

NO POSTAGE
NECESSARY
IF MAILED
IN THE
UNITED STATES

BUSINESS REPLY MAIL

FIRST-CLASS MAIL   PERMIT NO. 409   FREMONT, CA

POSTAGE WILL BE PAID BY ADDRESSEE

AUTOBAHN SYSTEMS, INC.

41027 Canyon Heights Drive
Fremont, CA 94539-9924